Against
the
Pollution
of the I

Against the Pollution of the I

Selected Writings of

Jacques Lusseyran

PARABOLA BOOKS

Against the Pollution of the I: *Selected Writings of Jacques Lusseyran*
© 1999 by PARABOLA Books

"The Blind in Society" and "Blindness, a New Seeing of the World"
originally appeared in *Proceedings,* Number 27.
"Against the Pollution of the *I* " originally appeared in *Proceedings,* Number 30.
These essays appear by permission of The Myrin Institute, Inc. for Adult
Education, 195 Main Street, Great Barrington, MA 01230.

"What One Sees Without Eyes" originally appeared in Jacques Lusseyran,
Ce que l'on voit sans les yeux (Paris: Cahiers de L'Unitisme, 1958).
Translation © 1999 by Rob Baker.

"Jeremy" and "Poetry at Buchenwald" originally appeared in Jacques Lusseyran,
Le Monde commence aujourd'hui (Paris: Editions de la Table Ronde, 1959). "Jeremy"
was first published in English in PARABOLA, Vol. 11, No. 2, "Mirrors."
"Poetry At Buchenwald" appeared in *The* PARABOLA *Book of Healing*
(New York: PARABOLA Books, 1994).Translations © Noelle Oxenhandler.

Published by the
Society for the Study of Myth and Tradition
656 Broadway, New York, NY 10012
www.parabola.org

Cover & Interior Design: Martin Moskof

06 05 04 03 02 01 00 99
10 9 8 7 6 5 4 3 2 1

Library of Congress Cataloging-in-Publication Data

Against the Pollution of the I : selected writings of Jacques Lusseyran.
    p. cm.
Contents: The blind in society—Blindness, a new seeing of the world—What one
sees without eyes—Against the pollution of the I—Jeremy—Poetry in Buchenwald
    ISBN 0-930407-46-6 (cloth : alk. paper)
    1. Lusseyran, Jacques. 2. Spiritual biography. 3. Vision—Religious aspects.
4. Prisoners of war—France Biography. 5. Prisoners of war—Germany Biography.
6. Blind—France Biography.
I. Title.
BL73.L87A3 1999
940.53'44'092--dc21
[B]   99-29783
                                                                                    CIP

Contents

Introduction

A FRIEND TELLS THE STORY OF A DUTCH GIRL, born deaf, whose parents decided to treat her no differently than if she had been born hearing. They spoke to her constantly, read fairy tales, sang lullabies and songs, played music for her. The girl grew up to be an exceptionally intelligent, happy woman. She speaks clearly, without the slurring common among the deaf. In a conversation, where she can lipread, an interlocutor would never guess that she is deaf. More remarkably still, this deaf woman, who today counsels the parents of deaf children, enjoys music and goes to concerts.

Evidently, we hear with more than our ears. What we hear is much more than bare acoustic information. The story of the Dutch girl puts in question whether we "hear" sound in the usual sense at all. When my friend said that the deaf girl's parents spoke to her, he meant that in their unconditional relationship, the parents sought—with intention and attention—to participate with their daughter in a world of *love and meaning*. Meaning is not abstract or intellectual, but real, a lived experience, at once cognitive, soulful (filled with feeling), and intentional. This is true of music as well as of the sounds of nature (birdsong, windbreath, waterfugue) which are harbingers of superhuman, cosmic meaning. But the question remains: if this deaf girl did not hear with her ears, with what organ or sense *did* she "hear"? We would be equally correct if we replied either "with her mind" or "with her body."

I say "either" because, to understand the world and our place within it, we must pass beyond the old dichotomies of body and mind, self and world, to a larger unity. "Inside and outside," Jacques Lusseyran writes, "have become inadequate concepts."

The poet Rainer Maria Rilke coined the

expression *Weltinnenraum,* "the inner space of the world." In an uncollected poem, he writes:

> What birds dive through is not
> the familiar space which heightens form for
>   you—
> there, in the free, you are denied,
> you disappear without return.
>
> Space grasps out of us and translates things:
> to realize the existence of a tree,
> throw *innerspace* around it, throw it out
>
> of the space that is in you. Surround it with
>   restraint.
> It is without boundaries. Only in the frame
> of your renunciation does it become truly *tree.*

Rilke also writes about a experience that occurred while he was walking up and down, reading a book outdoors at Duino (where he wrote the *Elegies*). Without thinking, he was moved to lean against a tree and remained rapt, absorbed by nature, in a state of what he calls "almost unconscious contemplation." Gradually, he noticed a slight sensation, an almost imperceptible vibration, passing into him from the interior of the tree. He writes that "he felt he had never before been filled with more delicate vibrations. His body was being treated in some sort like a soul, and made capable of receiving a degree of influence which could not really have been felt in the usual well-defined clarity of physical conditions." He could not distinguish through which sense this sensation was reaching him. After a while, he said aloud to himself, "I have reached the other side of nature." His body "became indescribably touching to him and of no other use than that he might be present in it." It was as if he were looking at the world from the other side, from a spiritual distance, where everything had an inexhaustible significance and an odd contingency. "He was looking back at things, as it were, over his shoulder, and a daring sweet flavor was added to their existence, now finished for him, as if everything had been spiced with a touch of the blossom of farewell." Later, trying to find analogues and precursors, he recalled a moment when in another garden "a bird call in the open and in his inner consciousness were one, when it did not as it were break on the barrier of his body, but gathered both together into an undivided space, in which there was only one region of the deepest consciousness, mysteriously protected."

Such is the world to which Jacques Lusseyran bears witness. He does so existentially, with his life, and phenomenologically, in that he allows his experience to speak for itself. For Lusseyran, it is a world that he discovered for himself and that discovered him; and it affected him with the full transformative power of a religious revelation. He became the voice of that world, speaking with the power and conviction of a new convert. It was a world, he insisted, not peculiar to him, but in fact the real and true world to which we all belong. Lusseyran gives us a miracle: a genuine act of self-discovery that is at the same time a universal reality. As if that were not enough, he was also a genuine twentieth-century "hero" or, viewed from another perspective, a "saint"—one of that select company of secular saints (others would be Simone Weil and Ludwig Wittgenstein) whose presence has sanctified our time and made it luminous.

Born in Paris in 1924, his childhood was exceptionally happy. As he tells it in his autobiography *And There Was Light,* his parents were ideal—generous, attentive, warm, protective, confidence-inspiring. In his own words, they were "heaven." Very early, they communicated to him the sense that "another Being" loved him, concerned itself with his life, and even

spoke to him. For his first seven years, Jacques Lusseyran lived a life of pure, unadulterated, childhood joy.
He loved everything in life, especially light in all its
manifold forms and colors, including darkness.

When he was seven, around Easter, something happened. It was time to go back to Paris from
the little village in the Anjou where he had been
vacationing. The buggy was at the door to take him
to the station. Inexplicably, he stayed behind in the
garden, by the corner of the barn, in tears. "I was crying," he writes, "because I was looking at the garden
for the last time." Three weeks later, at school, as
class ended, there was a rush for the door, a scuffle;
Jacques was taken off guard and fell. His head struck
one of the sharp corners of the teacher's desk. He
was wearing spectacles, one arm of which drove deep
into his right eye. He lost consciousness, and when
he came to, his eyes were gone. The doctors had
decided to remove the right eye, and the operation
was successful. As for the left eye, the retina was badly
torn too. The blow had been so severe as to cause
sympathetic ophthalmia. Jacques "had become completely and permanently blind."

But though Jacques became blind, he continued to see. After a few days, he realized that by

looking inward, he could see a *radiance*: "light ris-ing, spreading, resting on objects, giving them form, then leaving them." He was able to live in this stream of inner light which, like outer light, illuminated objects and people, giving them form and full color. There were times when the light seemed to fade, or disappear, but this was only when he was afraid or hesitated, doubted or began to calculate.

Lusseyran also began to understand that there was a world beyond the ordinary auditory sense, where everything had its own sound. These sounds were neither inside nor outside, but "were passing through him." Similarly with touch: a new world of infinitely differentiated pressure opened up to him. To find one's way around the world, all it took was a certain training in *attention*. Reality was a complex field of interacting pressures. "By the time I was ten years old," he writes, "I knew with absolute certainty that everything in the world was a sign of something else, ready to take its place if it should fall by the way. And this continued miracle of healing I heard expressed fully in the Lord's Prayer that I repeated at night before going to sleep...."

What accounts for this? Lusseyran gives no global explanation, except, as in the case of the

Dutch girl, to insist on the wisdom and the health of his parents' decision not to treat his blindness as a "disability" and sequester him from the world among the "disabled," but to allow him to continue to lead an ordinary life among the "seeing." He went back to school. When he learned Braille, his parents bought him a Braille typewriter. The rest was imagination, attention, and a deepening sense of the inner light. He was reborn.

Lusseyran was an extraordinary soul. A brilliant student, he quickly became the head of his class—a lively, joyful, reflective, deeply caring young person. He loved languages, literature, art, theater, life. Then, on March 12, 1938, Germany invaded Austria. The thirteen-year-old heard the news on the radio and heard the German language, twisted and tormented in unimaginable ways. To understand what he heard, he decided to perfect his German, for he intuited that what was happening would destroy his childhood.

When war broke out, he did not at first know whether it was his war or not. Its reality permeated his consciousness only "drop by drop, like the effects of hard liquor." Eventually he knew that it was. The family moved south to Toulouse. He was fifteen. He discovered love. But France was falling, Hitler was moving southward, exams were cancelled. There was confusion everywhere. On June 17, the collaborator Henri Philippe Pétain announced the surrender of France. The next day, Charles de Gaulle, from London, made his first appeal for resistance. There was no question as to which call Jacques Lusseyran and his friend, Jean, would respond.

The family moved back to Paris. The lycée reopened. Paris seemed to be praying. The young Jacques began to study philosophy, "from Pythagoras to Bergson, from Plato to Freud." "I tried all the avenues, one after the other," he writes. "All the way from Heraclitus to William James, no one of them seemed to me without function, but none satisfied me completely."

The turning point came when the Gestapo showed its hand. People began to disappear. Jacques fell ill with measles, and when it left him "it set free a torrent of energy." He formed his own Resistance movement. Fifty-two young people between the ages of seventeen and twenty-one attended the first meeting. Within a year, there were more than six hundred. Calling themselves the Volunteers of Liberty, they took it as their task "to give people the news"—

creating an information network, a newspaper. It is a miracle of the Resistance, this army of young people, commanded by a blind adolescent who kept everything, including fifteen hundred telephone numbers, in his head to avoid having anything incriminating on paper. Nor was that all; in the fall of 1941, he entered the University of Paris to study literature.

Fate's inevitable stroke came in July 1943: Lusseyran was arrested. His reflection on it in his autobiography is revealing:

> One small piece of advice. In a spot like this don't go too far afield for help. Either it is right near you, in your heart, or it is nowhere. It is not a question of character, it is a question of reality. If you try to be strong you will be weak....
>
> No, reality is not your character which, for its part, is only a by-product—I can't define it, a collection of elements. Reality is Here and Now. It is the life you are living in this moment. Don't be afraid to lose your soul there, for God is in it.
>
> Make all the gestures you like. Wash your hands if there is a place to wash them, stretch out on the ground, jump up and down, make a face, even shed tears if they help, or laugh, sing, curse. If you are a scholar—there is a gimmick for every category—do what I did that night.

> Reconstruct, out loud, Kant's arguments in the
> first chapters of his *Critique of Pure Reason*. It is
> hard work and absorbing. But don't believe any
> of it. Don't even believe in yourself. Only God
> exists.
>
> This truth, and it holds good always,
> becomes a miraculous healing remedy at such a
> time....

From July 22 to September 8, he was taken
thirty-eight times to be questioned by the Gestapo.
There was a certain amount of brutality. To survive,
he writes, he managed to forget their presence and
dwell in the depths, in the innermost sanctum, of his
being that was pure light. Then the SS changed the
subject, and the questioning came to an end. He was
sent to prison at Fresnes. In January, an SS lieu-
tenant came to his door and called his name. Was it
freedom or its opposite? They said he was lucky: they
were taking him to Germany. He had just spent a
hundred and eighty days in a cell, and he could hardly stand up. A nightmare journey followed, ending as
they drove through a monumental entrance with military bands drawn up on either side playing what
sounded like dance tunes. The inscription read *Kon-
zentrationslager Buchenwald*. He survived there for

eighteen months until liberated by General Patton. He has left us a vivid record of his Buchenwald experiences in "Jeremy" and "Poetry in Buchenwald." We will not forget.

The challenge with which Lusseyran confronts us is that these two realities of light and faith are ineffable and unstated realities. Faith must become an experience that unfolds "our very self." This is why I think it legitimate to call him a secular "saint," as well as a hero. What he has to say about his cognitive and suprasensory experiences is challenging enough. The world is other than what we seeing, sleeping ones imagine. He convinces us of the truth of this other world, even if we do not quite understand it. We realize that there is more than simply an altered, perhaps truer state of consciousness: Lusseyran is really talking about *metanoia,* a change of mind *in God.*

In "What One Sees Without Eyes," after describing his realization that he had lost nothing when he had become blind—that an inner light greater than any outer light had come to take the place of that which he had lost—he writes: "When one realizes that...I assure you it is not difficult to believe in God. He is there under a form that [is]...

quite simply alive.... When I remember it, I have exactly the sensation of someone taking my hand, or that a ray of light—it is exactly this way—comes toward and touches me. If I know where that ray of light is, I no longer have any problems."

This thought explains the crux of his insight. Attention, the thread that leads us from the labyrinth, is not only attention. It is the way we turn toward that ray of light so that it can come toward and touch us. It is the part of our relationship to God that depends on us. It is what connects us to reality. Another word for it could be presence, being present: wakeful, active receptivity. Anything that disturbs this presence must be avoided. One must strive for what the ancient monks called *apatheia,* detachment, and the German mystics, *Gelassenheit,* letting go. We must become blind again and again. Then the one who is seeing—what he calls "the essential power," "our link with the principle, with God"—can be present.

That is one side of Lusseyran: the mystic. This side is rarely evident in isolation. Lusseyran is not a cloistered monk, but a man of action, a human being in love with humanity—a man who loves human beings and is torn apart by their ignorance, foolishness, and inhumanity to each other. Therefore, he cannot help but talk to change the world. This is because, as he writes in "The Blind in Society," there is only one way to the inner light—love. For this inner life, which is life, *is* love.

Jacques Lusseyran is a fiery activist, a spokesperson for humanity, issuing an awakening call that does not discriminate on the basis of any physical "disability." "No blindness exists when it is a question of reflecting, intending, planning something, or even of helping people to live"—Lusseyran proved that. He has further shown that our disabilities, losses, griefs, and failings are gifts. We receive little deaths, if we are willing to die them, and live anew: "God wills it so. Order is restored. Nothing ever disappears completely." As for blindness: "if there is one realm in which blindess makes us experts, it is the realm of the invisible."

In addition to the mystic and activist, there is Lusseyran the phenomenologist of the senses. In a few sentences, he sketches a revolutionary, nondualistic anthropology. The human being as a whole is a sense organ, a nonmaterial perceiving being. All our senses are one: "the successive stages of a single perception, that that perception is always one of touch." We can understand what he means by touch when we realize

that what he means is "contact" and that the psychological form of primal contact is *attention*. We move
from being subjects for objects to becoming a space, a
field within which color, sound, smell—neither inside
nor outside—come to meet attention. Here, in this
field of vibration or force field, each object is and carries its own meaning. He apologizes: language can
take him no further. Yet it takes him very far, and
often in the simplest, most obvious direction. His last
paper, "Against the Pollution of the *I*" (he died on his
way to deliver it in Zurich) is especially moving. The *I*
he speaks of is but another name for the mysterious,
fragile, central *vitality*—the light, life, and love that
we are when we attend and open the possibility of a
true inner life. He sees this *I* under attack from every
side. He would have us wake up!

There is no more important function of a
writer in our time than to call us to awaken. The state
of siege under which human consciousness—human
conscience—lives has not abated in the time since
Lusseyran wrote. The seriousness of the situation has
only intensified. It is good to be reminded of what is
truly important, but only if we are willing to do something about it.

Christopher Bamford, January 1999

The Blind in Society

The long journey that brought me from the middle of the Pacific, and today gives me the pleasure of meeting you in Switzerland, took place on account of a book. I first wrote that book in my mother tongue, French, and called it *Et La Lumière Fut*. Then I published it in English in the United States and England. Finally it was translated into German, with the title *Das Weidergefundene Licht*. It is the story of my life or, rather, of what life taught me between the time when I completely and irrevocably lost the light of my eyes through an accident at the age of seven and a half, and the spring of 1945, when I came out

alive from Buchenwald concentration camp in Nazi
Germany.

And There Was Light is undoubtedly the most
personal of the books I have written—and the most
intimate. Yet it has given me the opportunity to establish contact with the greatest number of my fellow
men. This does not surprise me. Whenever we take
the trouble to plumb the depths of an experience and
extract from it all it contains, the simplest as well as
the most hidden, we cease to speak of ourselves and
ourselves alone. Instead, we enter the realm of the
most precious, the realm of universal experience,
which we share with all others.

I do not apologize, therefore, for telling you a
little more about myself today. What a man has discovered in his life—be it ever so unique—belongs to
all. If his discoveries can enhance and enrich the life
of others, it is his duty to speak of them.

Well, that is the case here. What thirty-seven
years of blindness have taught me—I must admit—is
to make great efforts. But they are much more than
efforts; they are also discoveries. I can hardly wait to
tell you about some of them.

Barely ten days after the accident that blinded
me, I made the basic discovery. I am still entranced

by it. The only way I can describe that experience is in clear and direct words. I had completely lost the sight of my eyes; I could not see the light of the world any more. Yet the light was still there.

It was there. Try to imagine what a surprise that must have been for a boy not yet eight years old. True I could not see the light outside myself any more, the light that illuminates objects, is associated with them, and plays on them. All the world around me was convinced that I had lost it forever. But I found it again in another place. I found it *in myself* and what a miracle!—it was intact.

This "in myself," however, where was that? In my head, in my heart, in my imagination? Don't you feel that such questions are purely intellectual, and worthy only of those adults who have already forgotten the utter simplicity and unquestionable power of true experiences? For me—I was in my eighth year and lived, instead of thinking—the light was there. Its source was not obliterated. I felt it gushing forth every moment and brimming over; I felt how it wanted to spread out over the world. I had only to receive it. It was unavoidably there. It was all there, and I found again its movements and shades, that is, its colors, which I had loved so passionately a few weeks before.

This was something entirely new, you understand, all the more so since it contradicted everything that those who have eyes believe. The source of light is not in the outer world. We believe that it is only because of a common delusion. The light dwells where life also dwells: within ourselves.

Yet I had to make the effort to find my way between doors, walls, human beings, and trees. As happens to all blind persons, I hurt myself often. But I quickly learned that I knocked against things only when I forgot the light. When I paid constant attention to the light, I ran a much smaller risk.

The second great discovery came almost immediately afterwards. There was only one way to see the inner light, and that was to love.

When I was overcome with sorrow, when I let anger take hold of me, when I envied those who saw, the light immediately decreased. Sometimes it even went out completely. Then I became blind. But this blindness was a state of not loving any more, of sadness; it was not the loss of one's eyes.

I spoke to you of discoveries. This was one of them, and it was so great that a whole lifetime full of religion and morality is often not enough to enable others to make it.

In another respect, too—I wish to say this here—I was exceedingly fortunate. I had parents who understood. Neither my father nor my mother ever pitied me because of my fate. They never said the word "unfortunate" in my presence. My father, who deeply understood the spiritual life, immediately said to me: "Always tell us when you discover something." I was to discover more and more! And he was right. One should not try to console either those who lost their eyes, or those who have suffered other losses—of money, health, or a loved one. It is necessary instead to show them what their loss brings them, to show them the gifts they receive in place of what they have lost. Because there are always gifts. God wills it so. Order is restored; nothing ever disappears completely.

I knew this when I was eight years old, because I had found the light again. From that moment on, blindness became for me a fascinating experience and the attempt to live a new way.

I could not read with my eyes any more. But what did it matter? I drew within myself letters and words on a canvas greater and more radiant than all blackboards, and within a few weeks I could learn to write again in Braille.

I saw neither sun, nor plants, nor the faces of

those around me with my eyes. But it was enough for the warmth of the day to touch me, for a tree to appear along the way, for a voice to call me, and immediately those beings and objects came to life on the inner canvas. All that remained was to learn a few simple techniques in order to tackle everyday problems—the only ones that could still be called difficulties: writing Braille, reading it as fluently as possible, typing on a regular typewriter because it was necessary to be able to establish direct contact with the seeing. All this I learned, fortunately, very early in life, between the ages of eight and ten.

My parents had decided, further, to let me stay among my seeing comrades. This was a bold decision. A special school for the blind would have offered greater guarantees, and I am still of the opinion that for most blind persons a special school is the quickest and most advantageous. Yet the necessity of living under the same conditions as everyone else has taught me a great deal.

I had to forget that I was blind. I had to stop thinking about it. I could compare my experiences with those of the others, and I understood very quickly that my blindness saved me from one great misery: that of living with egotists or fools. Only those who were capable of being magnanimous and understanding sought my company. It was much easier for me to choose my comrades. I never met the boys and girls who expect only personal gain from friendship, because they never came to me. So I met the best, first in public school, then at high school in Paris, without ever having to make an effort. They were there, close to me, with me. They asked me questions, and I asked them in turn. They helped me to live as if I had eyes, to learn to climb trees, to row a boat, and sometimes to steal apples. And to their surprise and often to my own, I taught them to see better.

Because of my blindness, I had developed a new faculty. Strictly speaking, all men have it, but almost all forget to use it. That faculty is attention. In order to live without eyes it is necessary to be very attentive, to remain hour after hour in a state of wakefulness, of receptiveness and activity. Indeed, attention is not simply a virtue of intelligence or the result of education, and something one can easily do without. It is a state of being. It is a state without which we shall never be able to perfect ourselves. In its truest sense it is the listening post of the universe.

I was very attentive. I was more attentive than any of my comrades. All blind persons are, or can be.

Thus they attain the power of being completely present, sometimes even the power of changing life around them, a power the civilization of the twentieth century, with its many diversions, no longer possesses.

Being attentive unlocks a sphere of reality that no one suspects. If, for instance, I walked along a path without being attentive, completely immersed in myself, I did not even know whether trees grew along the way, nor how tall they were, or whether they had leaves. When I awakened my attention, however, every tree immediately came to me. This must be taken quite literally. Every single tree projected its form, its weight, its movement—even if it was almost motionless—in my direction. I could indicate its trunk, and the place where its first branches started, even when several feet away. By and by something else became clear to me, and this can never be found in books. The world exerts pressure on us from the distance.

The seeing commit a strange error. They believe that we know the world only through our eyes. For my part, I discovered that the universe consists of pressure, that every object and every living being reveals itself to us at first by a kind of quiet yet unmistakable pressure that indicates its intention and its form. I even experienced the following wonderful fact:

A voice, the voice of a person, permits him to appear in a picture. When the voice of a man reaches me, I immediately perceive his figure, his rhythm, and most of his intentions. Even stones are capable of weighing on us from a distance. So are the outlines of distant mountains, and the sudden depression of a lake at the bottom of a valley.

This correspondence is so exact that when I walked arm in arm with a friend along the paths of the Alps, I knew the landscape and could sometimes describe it with surprising clarity. Sometimes; yes, only sometimes. I could do it when I summoned all my attention. Permit me to say without reservation that if all people were attentive, if they would undertake to be attentive every moment of their lives, they would discover the world anew. They would suddenly see that the world is entirely different from what they had believed it to be. All science would become obsolete in a single moment, and we should enter into the miracle of immediate cognition.

This immediate and complete cognition, I assure you, is not mine. The blind do not have it. Yet they have an additional chance when they try to approach it.

When I was seventeen, I graduated from high

school and entered college. But this was no longer essential. The false peace between the two wars had just come to an end. Europe had thrown itself into the worst conflict of its history, and my homeland, France, had been conquered within five weeks. Paris was occupied by the Nazis.

As you can imagine, I have often been asked how it was possible for me to participate in the Resistance and render valuable services to it. Even more frequent was the question why I, as a blind person, chose to do so. Let me explain it to you more simply than ever before.

During the first months of the occupation I experienced something like a second blindness. This happened although I was not a nationalist. Although the occupation of France was a shock to me, I thought about the oppression of Europe even more than of the terrible, all-embracing fact of the occupation. In addition, neither my family nor I were anti-German. I had studied German culture and the German language with awe and fascination. Yet I experienced this second blindness, the occupation by the Nazis, as I had the first.

Nine years earlier the outer light had been taken from me. This time outer freedom was taken

from me. Nine years earlier I had found the light
again in myself, intact and even strengthened. This
time I found freedom there, just as present and
demanding. Within a few weeks I understood that fate
expected the same work from me a second time. I had
learned that freedom was the light of the soul.

No one has the right to interfere with the free
will of men or with their self-respect. No one has the
right to murder in the name of an idea—still less in
the name of an insane idea. Reminding myself unceas-
ingly that freedom existed, and consequently reminding all those I met, had become for me the same
unquestionable duty as keeping alive the light behind
my closed eyes. There was no other reason for my
entering the Resistance movement. But there was the
difficulty of how to go about it.

I had already solved many problems, problems
related to my studies, intelligence, and inner life.
Now, however, I was faced with a very difficult one.
How could I find a place in the others' society, in
order to prove myself useful and necessary to them
and with them? A blind person would never be admit-
ted to a group of the Resistance. No one would be
able to visualize a place for him.

In the spring of 1941, therefore, I did what I

certainly never would have done so completely and so suddenly had I possessed the light of my eyes: I myself founded a Resistance group.

By taking the initiative I immediately rendered all prejudices invalid. By my decision alone I had proved that I was necessary. And that was not really difficult. Underground work required hands and eyes, but also courage and clear thinking. Also necessary was a *certainty* that did not depend on an idea, even an honest one, but on *experience* gained every day anew. This certainty I had.

Everything else came about as if by itself. I gathered around me several hundred young people, mostly students. We wrote and published an underground newspaper. We formed small action groups that one day could become the cadre of a national movement. As a matter of fact, at the beginning of 1943 I and six hundred of my comrades were finally able to join the *Défense de la France* movement, one of the five most important non-Communist Resistance groups.

I repeat: I am not sure I would have succeeded without my blindness. It was the *blind* leader whom all my comrades chose, and in whom they believed. From the first hour, I took full responsibility for enrolling new members. Each new applicant was introduced to me, and to me alone. I talked with him for a long time; I directed at him that special look which blindness had taught me. It was much easier for me than for anyone else to strip him of all pretenses. His voice expressed his inner being, and sometimes it betrayed him.

Finally I could make use of that inner life which fate had forced me to discover so early and so thoroughly. I used it to know better what I wanted myself, to realize what the others were capable of. The ability to join thoughts and feeling, to bring order into the world in my heart and my spirit without the help of objects, could finally be used for a task whose aims were outside myself. I know for certain that in more than two years none of my comrades ever thought of the limits blindness imposed on my work. I could neither carry arms nor run through the streets of Paris with a pack of underground newspapers over my shoulder, nor could I set out to discover a German military installation. My comrades went for me. But before they went they came to me to ask the way; afterwards they came again to report on their success, and it was my task to put the results in order and to decide on new actions.

In short—forgive me this statement, which I am making again without wanting to—I discovered that no blindness exists when it is a question of reflecting, intending, planning something, or even of helping men to live. And when in 1943 I joined, with my small forces, the *Défense de la France,* and suddenly was a member of its *Comité Directeur Clandestine* and was responsible for the distribution of a newspaper that appeared every two weeks in an edition of more than 250,000, no one around me was really surprised.

The test I was subjected to somewhat later was of an entirely different nature. In July 1943, I was arrested by the Gestapo. This happened, as it did with almost all Resistance fighters, because of a betrayal; without traitors, the Gestapo would never have been able to throw its net over a single underground organization. I was interrogated for forty-five days, kept in jail for six months, and in January 1944, taken to Buchenwald concentration camp. This time my fate was in no way extraordinary.

It is impossible to say in a few words what a concentration camp was, and I shall not attempt it. Is there a single person in Europe who does not already know? But I was not a prisoner like any other, because I was blind. I must tell you at least why I survived.

Of the two thousand Frenchmen who arrived in Buchenwald the day I did, only thirty were alive when the United States Third Army liberated the camp. That I am still here is one of those thirty miracles. My twenty-nine comrades cannot explain it any better than I can.

Yet I do not hesitate to say that I owe to my blindness more than to anything else that I was able to hold on. You must not understand this in a physical sense. When I succeeded in being tolerated in a camp where the Nazis systematically annihilated those whom they classified as "incapable of work," it was because I had found a way to make myself useful in the community of prisoners. I had become an interpreter. This was a real function. I was not an interpreter between the Nazis and my comrades—the Nazis ignored us except in the hours of destruction—but between my comrades themselves. In this international society, which lived in terror, it was very important to speak French, German, and later some Russian. I established communications, carried news; I listened to the mendacious news of the *Wehrmacht* high command, explained it to my comrades, deciphered it, corrected it. This activity assured me a place among them. I was no longer an invalid.

But that was not enough. In order to survive in a concentration camp, no ruse is sufficient. No form of intelligence is enough. When death is present every minute, when all those we love disappear, when humaneness vanishes, when no concrete reason any longer exists, nor a single sensible reason to hope, then an immediate refuge is necessary, an all-powerful refuge. And that is faith. Yet even the most fervent faith usually is no more than faith. A kind of faith is necessary that has its roots in our very being, that in time has become our very self. In other words, an *experience* is necessary. I had encountered that experience. Blindness had taught it to me one day.

I knew that when the light was taken from me, I could bring it to life again in myself. I knew that when love was taken away from me, its spring would flow again in myself. I even knew that when life is at stake, it is possible to find its source within oneself.

I know these are explanations that may seem abstract and that one does not live by theoretical solace. But for me they were not abstract. Every time the sight and the tests of the camp became unbearable, I closed myself off from the world. I entered a refuge where the SS could not reach me. I directed my gaze toward that inner light which I had seen when I was eight years old. I let it swing through me. And quickly I made the discovery that that light was life—that it was love. Now I could again open my eyes —and also my ears and nose—to the slaughter and the misery. I survived them.

If someone does not accept this explanation, which is the only correct one, then it seems to me that he does not know an all-important truth, namely, that our fate is shaped from within ourselves outward, never from without inward. Blindness, like any other great physical or moral loss, teaches this truth so thoroughly that in the end it is impossible to deny. Can I still call an accident that brought me such a gift "misfortune"?

Misfortune I met only later. What I call misfortunes here are the circumstances that our personal efforts cannot change, those which are imposed upon us by the prejudices of the majority and the indolence of those in power.

Let us never forget that the fate of the blind community is the fate of all minorities. It is of no importance whether these minorities are of national, religious, or physical origin. At the very best they are tolerated. They are almost never understood.

When the war ended, I returned to my homeland prepared to finish my studies and choose one of the professions for which I believed myself best qualified: diplomacy or teaching. But in 1942 the Vichy Government, in imitation of the Nazis, had enacted a new law. This law established the physical qualifications that were required of candidates for admission to the professions supervised by the government. It applied specifically to teaching and diplomacy.

Today this absurd law no longer exists. But seventeen years of unending effort were necessary to abolish it. And in those seventeen years I discovered the gulf that separates the seeing from those who do not have the light of their eyes.

I know that in this respect France showed a narrowness and stubbornness that does not exist in other countries. But the French example remains very meaningful. The seeing do not believe in the blind.

Their unjust and stupid doubt directed my actions during all those years. I decided not to fight the law directly, but to offer proof. I wanted to teach. I taught, so to speak, by force. I took it upon myself to teach without guarantees, without fixed employment, without pension rights, without pay during vacations.

I offered my services with persevering stubbornness. I asked only that they be judged by their value, instead of by what was *believed* to be their value. I carried on a long and lonely battle, which undoubtedly was the hardest of my life. Again, the story of my struggle is not my personal story; the struggle is the same one that all blind persons must fight.

I am convinced that the time has come to show the world what blindness really is. It is not an infirmity for which the afflicted constantly try to compensate according to their ability—that is, always incompletely. It is instead another state of perception. This state has its inherent practical difficulties. A blind professor needs a secretary to obtain the material he requires for his work. The blind manager of a trading company must be accompanied wherever he goes. But under modern conditions such obstacles are hardly noticeable. What lawyer, what engineer, even, could manage today without the help of a few competent assistants? Blindness is a state of perception which—when taken in all seriousness, accepted, and used—is capable of increasing many faculties sorely needed in every intellectual and organizational activity.

The memory of a blind man is better than that of a seeing person, given equal talent. And when we say "memory," we imply at the same time that other valuable ability: the ability to combine facts and ideas, to compare, to perceive new connections. There is no mystical reason for the better memory. It is simply that the blind in the course of time are forced to remember more than are the seeing. Thus a blind person, as I have frequently said, immediately discovers the all-powerful and entirely unexplored realm of attention.

In other words, he is less distracted by the world. Why not take advantage of this? Why shouldn't a blind person be assigned those tasks in the world that require his rare talent?

Let me make a practical suggestion. Since it is a fact that prejudices against the blind are strong, and prejudices are what human beings find most difficult to overcome, I would suggest the following rule: Every time a blind person applies for work, let us give him a chance. Let us employ him on probation. We could plan a probation of perhaps six or twelve months, during which the school, the office, or the firm that has hired him would be under no obligation. Nine out of ten blind persons have been denied employment not because they have proved themselves incapable, but because they have not even been permitted to furnish proof of their abilities. Let us allow them to work! Let us trust them for a while! The results would probably be amazing.

What I am suggesting is exactly what I achieved for myself. (Actually, we only really know what we have experienced ourselves.) It happened that I became a university professor in spite of my country's feudalistic laws, and I have pursued my profession for twenty-four years without encountering any difficulties except those connected with the profession itself.

I even dare to make the following statement: Teaching is often less difficult for a blind person than for a seeing one. When this point is disputed, the delicate question of discipline is always mentioned. But I ask you, are no seeing professors unable to command the respect of their students? It is obvious that discipline depends on the natural authority, the moral strength, of the teacher, on his ability to make his material come to life. Moral authority has nothing to do with having eyes.

I have been a teacher for twenty-four years without having encountered any difficulty caused by my lack of sight. As a matter of fact, the opposite is true. A lecture, a course, is an exercise of mind and character. It is based entirely on our ability to develop our inner life and to transmit it to others. In that respect blindness is a school without equal.

Why should it be necessary, when I stand before my students, to observe the position of their arms and legs? Why should I watch the vague expression of their faces, which convey only their lack of attention or their curiosity? Blindness has shown me a space other than the physical one, which only serves to separate me from them and them from me. This is the space where the stirrings of the soul and the spirit come into being. I know it from long practical experience. And silence, a certain quality of silence, shows me much better the degree of understanding, of interest, or of objection I cause in my students than could any enlargement of a movie showing their physical presence in slow motion.

What causes the failure of so many teachers today—and in Europe as well as in America much is made of that failure—is their inability to step out of their own heads. Many teachers are capable, many make praiseworthy efforts, but very few are able to enter the one realm where teaching can flourish. That realm is the common space between minds. Blindness has helped me there. I had for a long time practiced the techniques of an immediate exchange between human beings: the evaluation of voices, the evaluation of silence. Thanks to blindness I learned to read many signs that came to me from others, and that usually escape the notice of the seeing. If there is one realm in which blindness makes us experts, it is the realm of the invisible.

An audience is not an enemy for me; it is a new entity. Many new connections are suddenly formed within me. Since I cannot observe my audience with my eyes, and since I need not make the futile endeavor to divide it into single perceptions, it speaks to me as a whole, as a unit that can communicate.

I will not hide from you that I love my profession. It permits me every day to impart some of the unexpected, disquieting wealth that blindness has brought me.

I must come to an end. Can I add anything more? Perhaps it is this: If blindness is regarded as privation, it becomes privation. If we think of blindness as a deficiency that must be compensated for at any price, a path may open; but it will not lead far. If, however, we regard blindness as another state of perception, another realm of experience, everything becomes possible.

Continuing to see in their own way is undoubtedly all-important for the blind. I did not tell you that I have your eyes; I told you that I have other eyes. I did not tell you that my experiences are truer or more complete than yours. That would be a ridiculous presumption, even a lie. I said that the time has come to compare our experiences. When my wife paints, I ask her what her eyes see, ask her about all the lines they follow, all the colors they meet. At the same time, I paint within myself another picture. I know it is she who sees the physical picture, but I see it as well as she does. Isn't it a miracle that there are many ways of perceiving the world, not merely one?

Yes, you have heard me correctly: many ways of perceiving—but that very fact is our chance!

Blindness, a New Seeing of the World

This is my story. I saw, saw with my eyes, until I was eight years old. For more than thirty-five years now I have been blind, completely blind. I know that this story, this experience, is my greatest happiness.

I know, too, what one could say to this: These are only words; this is merely a poetic embellishment; it is a comforting fairy tale; it is mysticism; it is a proud rebellion against fate. This, however, is not true for me. I know too well that I did not attain this happiness by fighting for it, but that it has been given to me, and in a very natural way. I know, too, that it is not my privilege, my property, but a gift that I must accept anew every day, and that all the blind can receive in their own way.

I hope I shall be forgiven for starting with such a declaration of faith. But I cannot say anything about blindness that would be more important. I am thinking of the spiritual and practical help that it could give to all who share it.

And now I face a basic question. What value has seeing for us? What purpose does it serve? And I notice that no one has an earnest answer, neither the seeing nor the blind.

Well, this silence is quite natural. Why question something we own: life, sight?

Those who have sight do not think about it. Seeing to them is a simple act, an incontestable good. They might accept the warning of the philosophers who tell them: "Beware the delusion of the senses, and especially the delusion of the eyes!" But it is not seeing that is accused here, but the use that is made of it. Who will accept the validity of that other exhortation: "Close your eyes if you want to see"?

The blind, on the other hand, could ask themselves whether physical sight is deceptive, but they do not dare. They believe they do not have the right.

They do have some answers, but they hide them even from themselves. They bury deep in their consciousness what appears to them as mere dreaming. As far as the eyes' ability is concerned they share the opinion of the seeing, who daily make them believe it anew. The pressure of society—of those who see—weighs heavily upon them.

What is the value of seeing? Let me try to answer.

Seeing is a valuable sense. Those who are robbed of it know that very well. But seeing is primarily a practical sense. Seeing permits us to deal with shapes and distances. It makes every object useful, or at least usable.

Seeing presents itself to us as an extension of our hands, as an added ability to manipulate. Thanks to the eyes, we go forward. We make a greater part of the universe our own. We can operate even where our arms and legs do not reach.

We can make simultaneous observations through our eyes. When using them it is not necessary to know every object by itself, to measure things with the measure of our body. The eyes help us to many a beautiful victory over time and space. And that is the basic advantage of seeing; it places us in the center of a world that is much larger than we are.

But are these not the qualities of an instrument, or even a tool? Their advantages are obvious. But do they not depend entirely on the use we make of them? In short, does seeing have a power of its own, or is it nothing but a tool?

It is a very precious tool, and the blind who are deprived of it suffer a heavy loss. Yet it is only a tool, and therefore can be replaced. One of the greatest riches at our disposal is that there exist so many possibilities of sensual perception, that there is no unique or irreplaceable tool. Each sense can take the place of another, if it is used in its totality.

But now we are faced with a great difficulty, for seeing is a *superficial* sense.

It is often said that seeing brings us closer to things. Seeing certainly permits orientation, the possibility of finding our way in space. But with what part of an object does it acquaint us? It establishes a relationship with the *surface* of things. With the eyes we pass over furniture, trees, people, This moving along, this gliding, is sufficient for us. We call it cognition. And here, I believe, lies a great danger. The true nature of things is not revealed by their first appearance. I know that thinking can correct the information we receive through our eyes. But it is necessary to apply our thinking, and the whirl of daily necessities does not always leave us time to do so.

Seeing prefers outer appearance; this is part of its nature. It tends to regard consequences as causes. In our strange attitude toward the light we believe that our eyes see the sun, although they merely perceive lighted objects.

The danger, therefore, lies in the nature of seeing itself, in its quickness, in its usefulness. This is especially true when we use it for knowing other people. Think of the disastrous errors in our judgment when we base them on the clothes, the hairdo, and the smile of the person we meet. And yet the greatest part of our loving and our hating, as well as the greatest part of our opinions, depend on these clothes, on this smile.

A person approaches us. What does he mean for our eyes? First of all, he makes a physical impression: *i.e.,* there exists no relationship—not even a fleeting one—between him and us. There is only one between society and him, since it is obvious that clothes, smile, facial expression, even gestures, in a word, behavior, are the common property of society.

I think of the endless game, a game that has

become involuntary. We play it to call attention to ourselves. It is the art of deceiving the eyes of the other person, an art that fills many minutes of our lives. What we deceive is the eyes. For them we work. We know very well that they will pass over us quickly and not examine us very long.

Naturally, there are eyes that examine and do not merely see. They are the eyes of a mother or an anxious wife, the eyes of a good physician, or a wise man, an artist, and—why not?—of a humorist. But why is it that the moment these eyes see, they seem half closed and turned inward?

This process has many names: thinking, concentrating, reflecting. When we really think about it, however, we understand that it is always a protection against seeing. After we have received pictures through the eyes, it is necessary to hold onto these pictures, to explain them to ourselves without any visual support, in short, to give them an entirely new form of existence: the inner existence. Without this willingness to give up, at least temporarily, the impressions we receive through the eyes, no true cognition is in my opinion possible.

This simple fact should warn us of a momentous illusion: the illusion that forms are all-powerful.

Human beings primarily collect. They dream of increasing facts and experiences unendingly. If they want to learn about the world of plants, to determine differences and similarities, they differentiate and classify. To enumerate and classify forms has become the most important function of intelligence. What is true of systematic research is also true in our daily life. For most people, traveling means seeing everything: *all* landscapes, *all* rooms of a building. He who did not see all the rooms of a house, did not see the house. He who did not see all lawyers, all workers, did not see the man who is called lawyer or worker. That is the basic principle of all encyclopedias, of all lexicons, of nearly all textbooks. In this manner historical research is pursued, research into man and research into nature. And then we are surprised at its being insufficient and inadequate.

I believe that seeing is responsible for the prevalent conviction that we shall understand and completely recognize the world when we progress from one form to the next, from one phenomenon to the other. We forget that the motion itself, which leads the eyes from object to object, cannot take place in our eyes. It necessarily precedes and directs their movement.

Today, these observations take on an entirely new importance because our present world of posters, neon signs, movies, and television is based entirely on the reliability of the eyes. It has been said very correctly that we now live in the age of pictures. Isn't even the process of transmitting thoughts on the verge of being reduced to external pictures? Aren't we seeking a way to base teaching entirely on visual impressions? That a blind person should speak up and warn the seeing to be cautious about the use of their own eyes, as I am doing, may appear unseemly and even comical. Yet it is not the process of seeing that I attack.

I accuse only a certain idol worship. The idol is the conviction that seeing is the principal activity of the spirit, and sufficient for it.

Naturally, one cannot blame the eyes. On the contrary, they are so good that they should be improved even further.

What simply has to be understood is that seeing is not the work of the eyes alone. The ability to see must exist before its physical instrument, the eyes, can act. As long as men forget this fact, they will ever and again face illusion and failure. They will be impatient. They will want to see ever more and more.

And they will no longer know who it is that is confronted with such a flood of impressions and sees them.

All this is known to a blind person. He knows it naturally, not because of an extraordinary gift of intelligence or by his own merit. Deprived of the privilege of the eyes, he measures at the same time his loss and his gain. Most of all, he continues to live and to experience with an irresistible force the wonderful mutual exchange that takes place between the inner and the outer worlds.

This continuity in life is always granted us by God. When we experience a wall, a loss, a misfortune, it is not God who erected this wall, but our spirit. It has stepped outside the everlasting creation. It has preferred to the universal current of power its own current of power, so to speak. There it has stopped.

In reality, there is neither a wall nor a loss. Everything is replaceable and continuous. So it is with the light for the blind.

I listen with ever-renewed surprise when the most earnest people—physicians, writers, psychologists—talk of the terrible "night" into which blindness pushes us. "Night" is the word everyone uses. I must protest against it because this word reveals a strange judgment, a prejudice, or simply a superficial opinion. How is it possible, especially for a physician or a psychologist, not to suspect at least the principally relative character of all perception?

The facts are quite different from everything one generally imagines. To cease seeing with one's eyes does not mean entering a world in which light has ceased to exist.

What dwells in the head of a blind person is the light. Should we say in his head, or in his heart? Or perhaps even in his eyes? What difference does it make? The light is neither within nor without, but encompasses the whole being and wipes out the barriers we have created out of habit. The light is here! That is the only certainty.

I can foresee the objection that could be raised: Isn't your experience a deception? Once you could see, knew colors and forms. You could name them. But how is it with one who was born blind?

I admit, this is a weighty objection. It would be even more so if we lacked the testimony of the blind from birth who were healed. All claim, certainly, that the light, as it revealed itself to their eyes, was a surprise to them, a new discovery. But they confess at the same time that before they could see with their eyes they carried within themselves a counterpart of this light.

And so all is light in this blindness; and what is more, this manifest luminosity contains a magnificent lesson. Since my childhood I have been impressed with a phenomenon of surprising clarity: The light I saw changed with my inner condition. Partly it depended on my physical condition, for instance fatigue, restfulness, tension, or relaxation. Such changes, however, were relatively rare. The true changes depended on the state of my soul.

When I was sad, when I was afraid, all shades became dark and all forms indistinct. When I was joyous and attentive, all pictures became light. Anger, remorse, plunged everything into darkness. A magnanimous resolution, a courageous decision, radiated a beam of light. By and by I learned to understand that love meant seeing and that hate was night.

I had the same experience with space. When I became blind, I found out that an inner space existed. This space also changed its dimensions in accordance with the condition of my soul. Sadness, hate, or fear not only darkened my universe, but also made it smaller. The number of objects I could encompass within myself with one glance decreased. In the truest sense of the word, I knocked against everything. Objects and beings became obstacles within myself. Outwardly I could not avoid running against doors and furniture. I was punished very thoroughly and very quickly.

Conversely, however, courage, attention, joy, had the immediate effect of opening up and illuminating space. Soon everything existed in me abundantly: a great many objects, pictures, beings. I saw a magnificent landscape before me. I knew that this landscape could be expanded indefinitely; in order to achieve this, my joy had merely to become even greater. At the same time, my physical adroitness increased; I found my way and moved with assurance.

In short, there were two possibilities: to reject the world—and that meant darkness, reverses—or to accept it, and that meant light and strength.

I do not believe that my explanations contain anything particularly new, unless one takes into account the experimental, concrete, and sense-transmitted character of the facts described. The discovery made possible by blindness is undoubtedly the experience of the existence of an inner life. From numerous meetings with blind persons, and numerous questions put to them, I have learned that others have had similar experiences. Yet most do not talk about them.

In order to describe these experiences, certain technical faculties are required. It is necessary to master a certain language, that of psychology, and to practice a certain kind of analysis. But that is not of great moment, and many blind persons have this knowledge at their disposal.

We all know to how great an extent our experiences, especially inner ones, depend on language. Language, however, is first of all a collective tool. It may be said that it is the tool of the majority.

The words the blind use are the words of the seeing. They have borrowed them all, and the seeing do not take it too kindly that the blind make such positive use of their words. The seeing are given to intolerance.

A blind man is disabled; he is infirm; he is excluded from society and not counted a full person. He is accorded compassion, even help, but nearly everyone prefers to hear him complain about, rebel against, and accuse his being different, rather than to hear him describe with assurance the world he carries within himself. The blind often feel very painfully the doubt and lack of faith with which their personal experience is received.

The blind, therefore, either withdraw from the world and lead a life filled with strange habits, thereby widening the gap between themselves and the world of the seeing even more, or they direct their efforts toward making others forget their blindness. Rarely, very rarely, do they present themselves as blind, and as wishing to carry out their function as blind persons.

I believe that blindness *has* its own function. It has the tasks of reminding us that the despotism of one sense, sight, is unjust, and of cautioning us against the form of perception prevalent today. And, further, it is the task of blindness not only to recall to memory the origin of all knowledge, but also to remind us of the wonderful gift that permits a mutual exchange between other forms of perception and perceived pictures.

The blind know from direct experience that the *act* of seeing has priority over seeing in the usual sense, outer seeing. I consider it important that they do not hide this knowledge.

I consider it especially important that the blind and the seeing compare what they see. They should get together before they pass judgment, before they establish an order of rank for inner and outer seeing; they should compare their experiences, become aware of their mutual wealth of experience. And they should, one as well as the other, accept their limitations. I am convinced that this comparison would accomplish valuable work. I am convinced that after such an exchange of thoughts, the limits of both kinds of perception, limits that should be known, will stand out in new clarity. Let us hope that this dialogue will be candidly carried out some day!

I believe, however, that even today a preliminary listing of the gifts of the blind is possible. It is generally said that the loss of seeing immediately causes the other senses to develop further, that a compensation takes place. This is true. It is true that the blind hear better than the seeing. Sounds make it possible for them to perceive distances and even figures.

The shadow of a tree on the road is not only a visual phenomenon. It is also audible. The oak, the poplar, the nut tree have their own specific levels of sound. The tone of a plane tree is entered like a room. It indicates a certain order in space, zones of tension, and zones of free passage. The same is true of a wall or a whole landscape.

All differences in light have corresponding differences in sound. What I hear, while leaning out of my window under a gray, overcast sky, is sluggish. Sounds have become weak. They move in disconnected small groups. They circle in a single plane of space. What I hear when the sun shines has a much more intense vibration. Real objects emitting sounds begin to appear. The sounds go where they may, meet in accordance with their affinity, and combine into forms.

A blind person hears better, and that is as it should be, because he hears what he does not see. A blind person has a better sense of feeling, of taste, of touch. He should be told how much his senses keep in reserve for him. But first of all, it seems to me, it is necessary to point out to him the condition that leads to such a widening of the senses.

This condition isn't simply not seeing any more. Neither does it mean that a new structure is given to the remaining senses. The necessary condition is much simpler: one has to be attentive. A really attentive person could understand everything. For this understanding he would need nothing that is tied to the senses. Neither light, nor sound, nor the shape peculiar to every object would exist for him, but every object would reveal itself to him in all its possible facets. In other words, he would enter completely into its inner world.

The senses would continue to exist, because their role as natural intermediaries has been established by the order of creation itself. But they would no longer work independently, separated from each other, as we have wrongly assumed they must.

From just this "total attention" the seeing are constantly diverted. So are the blind, but not to the same degree. For them remaining attentive is a practical necessity, and this simple fact constitutes the first of their gifts.

Hearing, sense of smell, sense of touch! Truly, I hesitate to make these differences because I am afraid they are arbitrary.

Does a blind person really know what he perceives when, walking along on the sidewalk, he suddenly indicates that he has recognized a gap in the wall or building? Or when he stops a few inches before reaching an obstacle, without even having brushed against it? Can he put into words what he has experienced? I think not. He will say, when asked, that he heard something: less resonance, a movement of the air, like the very slow approach of an object. But this explanation is only a concession to the generally used language.

He did not hear. He touched. Perhaps hearing

and touch are the same sense perception. His ability to indicate the gap in the wall means that the free area of cement or stones had already taken possession of his whole body; with the whole surface of his body he had experienced its shape and power of resistance. It even means that he had already passed through the gap.

All our senses, I believe, join into one. They are the successive stages of a single perception, and that perception is always one of touch. Therefore hearing can replace seeing, and seeing can replace touch. Therefore no loss is irreparable.

At this point I ask myself whether what we call *attention* could be the psychological form of this fundamental contact, a form based on feeling as well as intellect. In other words, could attention be a kind of touch?

A blind person is in a room; a man enters, sits down, and does not talk. Can the blind person come to know him? Common sense will say no. But I am not sure that common sense is right. The blind person can strain his attention. He can open himself to such an extent that this unmoving person comes closer. By and by, quietly and without moving, he can remove all the inner obstacles that separate him from the other until he begins to absorb the man's appearance.

I know that such an experience verges on the limits of cognition. I know that it almost never takes place consciously. Yet I believe that every blind person has had it, whether he was conscious of it or not.

How can this be explained? Has the blind man developed a higher faculty? With the help of the spirit has he transcended the normal conditions of perception? I believe one should simply say: He touched.

I used a blind person as an example. I could equally well have spoken of a seeing person, because—to repeat—the special merit of blindness is not that it creates a different experience, but that it leads us by necessity toward a heightened experience.

Some have called this fundamental touch "a sense for obstacles." They have even tried to assign to it a certain part of the body. Some, in accordance with the tradition of esoteric physiology, have placed it in the region of the forehead, in the "eye of Shiva." Others, following a purely rational hypothesis, have spoken of cooperation of a mixture of elemental sense impressions of a visual character, located primarily in certain parts of the skin. This is the famous thesis of Jules Romains, laid down in his memorandum on "para-optical seeing," or "the sight that takes place outside the retina."

I, for one, would rather confine myself to a more direct observation.

What the blind person experiences in the presence of an object is pressure. When he stands before a wall he has never touched and does not now touch, he feels a physical presence. The wall bears down on him, so to speak. An effluvium emanates from that wall. Conscious perception takes place the moment it meets another effluvium, which originates in him.

Perception, then, would mean entering into an equilibrium of pressure, into a force field. As soon as we pay attention to this phenomenon, the world comes to life in a surprisingly different manner. No single object, no single being remains neutral. The oneness of the world is experienced as a physical event.

The pressure I have spoken of assumes all forms: absorption, transference, cooperation. Everything enters into an intimate and active relationship with ourselves: the window, the street, the walls of the room, the furniture, the slight movement of the air, living creatures. Finally, even thoughts take on weight and direction.

This is the experience of the blind, but—of this I am convinced—it is also a common experience. Seeing persons also experience these pressure effects, but they do not permit them to enter their consciousness. Yet it seems to me they could throw light on a great many rather vague but important states of mind: sympathy, antipathy, the feeling of being ill at ease, good will, the wish to stay or flee, opposition, devotion.

These conditions are always explained psychologically: I consider them to be much simpler.

I said "pressure." I said "effluence." I could also have expressed myself differently and talked about "a field of vibration." It is this basic vibration, which shapes objects and reveals beings, to which we are led by blindness.

To carry this analysis further does not seem desirable, because we have entered the realm of personal experience. When we wish to make our experiences known to others, the only way to do so is to explain and explain again, in complete detail.

I wished to call attention to the strangely one-sided character of our psychology of perception. The prejudice that arbitrarily elevates seeing to its all-powerful position has hidden from most thinkers that which makes possible seeing, as well as all other sense perceptions, and, more generally, our relationship to the world.

For all these reasons a blind person has the right to say: Blindness changed my sight, but did not extinguish it.

And now I hope that you will find it easier to accept my paradox, the confession of faith I made in the beginning: Blindness is my greatest happiness! Blindness gives us great happiness. It gives us a great opportunity, both through its disorder and through the order it creates.

The disorder is the prank it plays on us, the slight shift it causes. It forces us to see the world from another standpoint. This is a necessary disorder, because the principal reason for our unhappiness and our errors is that our standpoints are fixed.

As for the order blindness creates, it is the discovery of the constantly present creation. We constantly accuse the conditions of our lives. We call them incidents, accidents, illnesses, duties, infirmities. We wish to force our own conditions on life; this is our real weakness. We forget that God never creates new conditions for us without giving us the strength to meet them. I am grateful that blindness has not allowed me to forget this.

I should like to have this attitude called "optimistic," though optimism is not regarded highly today. This is my wish because I cannot admit that an experience is worthless because it is a happy one.

The blind see in their own way, but they do see. This is a fact that entails just as many risks and obligations for the blind as seeing does for those who are able to use the light of their eyes.

How much remains inside you,
and how much can you draw upon
from your own depths?
—Meister Eckhart

A person without an inner life
is a person with nothing added:
an empty sack which
therefore cannot be filled
and cannot remain standing.
—Johannes Tauler

*What
One
Sees
Without
Eyes*

Something has astonished me for a long time. It is that blind people never speak about the things they see. At least I never hear them talk about them to those who see with their physical eyes.

Rather often, however, when blind people are together, suddenly they tell each other what they perceive. Then why do they ordinarily keep quiet about this?

I think that basically the reason is rather simple. They keep quiet because of society. To live in society one must at any cost resemble everyone else. Society demands it. In order to adapt to the world of

the seeing, blind people are obliged to declare themselves unable to see—and, believe me, I know what
I'm talking about, for that has happened to me even
when I knew very well that it didn't correspond to
reality and was not true.

Therefore tonight, excuse me for not saying
to you a single time that I am blind. I will not speak
to you about blindness, but about its opposite.

To begin with, I have a very strong memory:
something which stays alive for me as an experience
every minute, but which presents itself to me, when I
think about it, as a memory. It is what happened to
me when I became blind at the age of eight.

I believed—oh, I believed, and with a great
dizziness, as you may well imagine, despite my young
age—that from the moment I lost my eyes, I would
from then on never see again. And then that was not
true. What a surprise! I still haven't forgotten it. I verified immediately and in a concrete way that I had not
lost anything, or rather that what I had lost was of a
practical order, and only of that order.

Oh, indeed, I could no longer walk around
freely; I had to be accompanied. I was sometimes
obliged to ask others for help—those who saw with
their eyes, who were passing around me. But the oth-

ers responded to me. Usually they responded very well. I learned very quickly that this was not very serious. No, truly, I had lost nothing at all.

What does this mean?

It does not mean that the situation must be explained in a moral manner or by poetic images—I will adamantly insist on that.

It means uniquely positive, concrete, and elementary things.

I had rediscovered inside myself everything which others described as being outside of us: on the exterior. And I verified for myself that they were wrong. They said, "But he can no longer see the light," or even, "If he says that he sees it, he is actually imagining it or remembering it." And people spoke to me of the marvelous memories I must have of the time when I could see. Or of the faculty that I possessed, as they put it, to an extraordinary degree: imagination. But, for my part, I was obstinately resolved not to believe them. I knew very well that I was not "imagining things." I knew that I was perceiving, that I was sensing.

Inside me was everything I had believed was outside. There was, in particular, the sun, light, and all colors. There were even the shapes of objects and the distances between objects. Everything was there, and movement as well.

I verified that sometimes the shapes I perceived inside myself were not exactly like those which others described to me. There were slight differences, little divergences. For example, a friend who had eyes told me that a wall at the side of the road was still quite a ways away from us, that it was about ten meters distant. Rather strangely, I felt it much closer. And then, several years later, I understood where the difference came from: The wall was very large and very tall, much taller than the other walls in the neighborhood. So nothing had really changed for me. My blindness did not prevent the wall from being a wall. It didn't change its being strong, solid, and immobile along the side of the road.

This is how things went for me right from the beginning, and it was and still is amazing to me.

From the moment I became blind, I did not enter a world of privations supported by courage, to "see" heroically what others described to me. Not at all.

I entered a world of enchantment, but an enchantment which supported my life, which nourished me, because it was real. It was not an imaginary fairy-tale enchantment, and I sensed that clearly.

And now, at the interior of this positive enchantment, I found a small understanding which was immediately a very great prize for me which I treasure to this day: the nature of light.

I knew very well that most of those who see with their eyes—I hardly dare call them "the seeing," for there would be an unpleasant ambiguity to that—usually say that light comes to them from the outside, that they catch it like a ball which is thrown to them.

I know very well that is not true. I know the nature of light is not to be outside of us, but, on the contrary, within us.

Exactly what is this nature of light? I could not tell you. I don't know. I only know how it really manifests itself. It is an element that we carry inside us and which can grow there with as much abundance, variety, and intensity as it can outside of us. Maybe even more intensely, and in a more stable, better balanced way, inside rather than outside.

There was this phenomenon that surprised me: I could choose when the light came or went. Yes, I could make it appear or disappear. I had that astonishing power: I could light myself. You heard right:

"light myself." That is to say, I could create a light inside me so alive, so large, and so near that my eyes—oh, it was very strange—my physical eyes, or what remained of them, vibrated, almost to the point of hurting, just as yours would hurt if you suddenly fixed them on the sun's ray too attentively. I could in the same way extinguish all, or almost all, light impressions, or at least reduce them, soften them into a monotonous gray, a sort of obscurity, whether pleasant or disturbing. In any case, for me the variations of light no longer depended on external phenomena—do I need to repeat that medically I was one hundred percent blind?—but on my own decisions.

All my childhood was sustained by these experiences and inclined—as you already must understand—toward joy. Not toward consolation—I have never needed to be consoled—but toward joy.

By all this, I learned at the same time that we should never give way to despair, that no matter what brutal and negative events occur in our lives, just as quickly the same sum of life is given back to us; that actually everything in the universe adds up to continuity. I no longer saw with the eyes of my body, as men of letters say, but with the eyes of my soul.

To tell the truth, I hardly need to involve my soul, because for me it was something much more direct, a great deal more physical, and quite simple.

Yes, there was continuity: I had lost nothing. I had been given as much as I had had taken from me, perhaps more.

When one realizes that, when one knows it from the age of nine or ten, I assure you it is not difficult to believe in God, because God is there. He is there under a form that has the good luck to be neither religious, nor intellectual, nor sentimental, but quite simply alive. And that is an extraordinary support for all the rest of life. I would sometimes forget that—I forget it even today—but that support remains alive. And when I do remember it, I have exactly the sensation of someone taking my hand, or that a ray of light—it is exactly this way—comes toward me and touches me. If I know what the ray of light is, I no longer have any problems.

Since becoming blind, I have paid more attention to a thousand things, and that this has allowed me to discover all sorts of aspects of the world that I probably would never have known otherwise. And these aspects are very comforting. They give life to everything. I'd like to give you some examples.

First of all, I perceived that sounds were not produced just by vibrating objects, but more generally, by all objects which make up our world, even those that we deem immobile or lifeless.

I observed, for example, that the wall which is here behind me also produces a sound. I say: "produces a sound."

Is it really a sound that I perceive in placing my attention on the wall? I'm not completely certain. But it is, if you wish, a shaking, something very light, but something repeated endlessly. I would say that it repeats as long as the wall stays behind me, exerting some force on my body.

Thus, the most apparently lifeless objects carry with them a potential for life as great as those which whirl and vibrate a lot—or are the most human.

What difference is there between a human voice and a tree's voice? Very slight, unless you have acquired the habit of understanding the human voice more rapidly than a tree's voice. But both are one voice.

I remember this experience. I've retold it often to my friends, it's so pleasant.

I discovered as a child that different species of trees don't have the same presence. In particular,

I did not experience the same sensations when I passed along a street shaded by an oak tree that I did going down one shaded by a fir tree or an acadia.

During vacations in the country, when I had made friends with the landscape during the long weeks, I could distinguish the tree under which I passed by its volume, its configuration, the distinct sound of its shadow.

That's only one detail. But there are a number of details like that. And that's why, when I found myself in the presence of an unknown mountainous landscape, when I was still hundreds of feet or even a few miles away from the neighboring summits, I could give a general indication of their silhouettes! It was as if I saw them: I saw far beyond me the great outlines and shapes of the mountains. How did I know what they looked like? I knew absolutely nothing about them. Nonetheless they appeared to me—or, more precisely, I verified them within myself, exactly as I verified the presence of light.

Once again: I did not have to leave my armchair, I did not have to move, because things were inside me.

I began to verify that most of the particular sensations that I experienced and that I attributed just now to hearing, touch, or smell, always related essentially to the same sort of sensation.

I'm about to give it a name, which may not be a very good idea: a sensation of pressure.

The universe had weight and was always pressing against me. Which is to say that it presses equally against you.

All the objects in the universe seem to be masses of energy located somewhere, and it doesn't matter much where, except on the level of mechanics pure and simple: physical relationships.

Therefore, these masses of energy exist somewhere and draw near or far, making an impression on us, the whole affair being one of perception for us.

I mention again the example of the walls of this room.

The four walls of this room lean against me. Their life consists—to the extent that their life concerns me—of leaning on me from a certain distance.

Or preferably: I also lean on them. Yes, I lean on them by the simple fact, for example, that I think about them.

I think about the four walls of this room, simultaneously of these four walls. It is as if one of my hands were propped up against that wall on the right, and the other against the wall to the left, and two more against those in front of or behind me. It is as precise as that.

And it still seems that the walls exist as a point of encounter between these two pressures: that coming from them and that coming from me.

It seems almost that the walls are the conjunction, the union of these two forces, their equilibrium; I almost want to say their reconciliation.

I think that you feel to some extent that these remarks of mine are, if not surprising, at least difficult to express. Well, that's because we have the habit—and a very bad habit—of believing things are outside of our control, that they either come to us or don't, that they are stubborn as mules, that we will never be able to make them do what we want. Translation: that we are poor unfortunates, creatures forgotten by the universe, and that we—free, generous and heroic beings—cannot obtain the responses from things which we feel are our due.

That's true: we are in a battle against things. But it's not the things' fault. It would be so simple to catch them where they live and not somewhere else—and that place where they live is not outside.

What role does blindness play in this affair?

The answer is so simple that it's right under our nose. Blindness leads us to perceive more clearly, more immediately the connections between objects and the universe at large. Then we make some big discoveries.

So, as I was saying, objects exert pressure on us. We exert another pressure on them, or at least it seems that that's the way it is. And the world—of real spectacles, real images—is produced by the encounter of these two movements, at the same time.

When one knows this fact, when one thinks about it a little, the proportions of the universe change. One perceives a solidity, a new resonance.

There are echoes everywhere. There are presences everywhere. There is a rather marvelous exchange going on: between the concave and swollen, the full and the empty, between the explosive and the responsive. One doesn't have to touch a statue with one's fingers or the palm of the hand to know the statue.

That is what I want to say.

You know that your eyes are a very useful sense organ, for with them you can travel in an instant to numerous places, to numerous points on the surface of objects.

You can go very quickly, with your eyes. You can glide. Excuse me; I don't want to scold or insult you, but I am obliged to say to you: you glide too quickly.

This ends up becoming a frightening temptation for you.

Fingers don't glide.

With my fingers I can know this table. I am obliged to feel my way around it. That is to say, I make my fingers explore all its parts, one after another, until at last I know it all, completely. For indeed, if I have touched a smooth part on the left side of the table, I cannot yet know if I am going to find a big hole in the middle of the table. Why not? Maybe there is a hole. I will know it only when I come into tactile simultaneity with it. The touch gives the proof.

But it is possible, without eyes, to apprehend a part of an object and to know it immediately, instantaneously, in its entirety.

It is possible for a blind person to hear the voice of a man or woman speak just three words to recognize that man or woman as if they had been speaking for hours. How is that possible?

Is it really necessary that the blind person be a first-rate psychologist in order to have this facility, or have made long and detailed studies of human mechanics? Do you think so? It is sufficient, as always, to be attentive.

The part is equal to the whole. The hand conveys the arm. The arm conveys the whole body. The body conveys the past, present, and future actions of whoever inhabits it.

There is another thing to which the blind person becomes habituated very quickly, if you want to so much as give it a thought.

And what does it prove, this brief experiment, if not that things and people are not outside of us to discover and explore, but on the contrary that we already carry things inside of ourselves. They are there in advance. We require only a little shock, a very brief opportunity—just a flicker of movement or the sound of their voice, in order to perceive their presence.

All these things are naturally true for those who see, just as for those who don't see.

All that is a question of attention—and a question of the direction taken by us inside ourselves

Basically blindness gives a great force, that of discovery that the inner life is not at all what people imagine it to be.

When people speak of the inner life, they irresistibly—and one must add bizarrely—think of I don't know what construction, what imaginary fabrication: perhaps, a novel. That's the simplest word of all. Indeed, there are certainly some very good novels. There are those which give the illusion of reality and those which don't do that at all. There are good craftsmen of the inner life—and bad ones. That is what the majority of people believe—and they take you for a great rogue if you seriously say to them that you have a real inner life—"Ah, well, that fellow, he invents things! He comforts himself as best he can! He is rather clever!" At the very least they laugh at you, which happens very often, and accuse you of not adapting to the modern world.

Well, it's not that way at all.

It is incontestable that certain inner lives are entirely fabricated, unfortunately. These are fictitious lives, and God knows what there is to them.

The true inner life either is or is not.

If it is, it is not absolutely different from external life. It does not oppose it. It is not in battle against the necessities of positive existence: it contains exactly the same things as external life. Only this time they are seen and perceived from within.

I have said here at least a good dozen times, "within us" or "within me."

So what does that ultimately mean?

For as long as one merely uses the expression, one is still in the world of language: with a meaning that is banal, loaded.

What is the "inside" that is inside us? And consequently, what is this "inner" of inner life?

Is it necessary to represent things as if we were a husk, a large shell which, like all shells, has at its center a space which is more or less empty or full?

And is it true that a blind person very often sees things as if he were lightly separated from them, as if only one part of them were available to him, the other parts remaining on the surface, which can only be scratched or grazed, not penetrated?

Sensations like this exist.

But to a very perceptible degree, this sensation of the husk or shell disappears.

And things are there, without space.

Yes, "without space."

You ask me: Is that possible? Have you found the recipe for inner life?

Alas! How could I explain to you? I hardly know what it is.

No. I know simply that things are there, are present, without having to attribute to them a particular position in the world.

When you look with your eyes, you say: "This ashtray is there, in front of me, just to my right." "That man or woman is over there; I see him or her in a precise position that is such and such in relationship to the neighboring position." You take into account the space and you imagine to yourself that the space you have imposed can not be destroyed, that in fact it exists, is substantial.

But, for experiential reasons once again, I think that is not true.

If, speaking from the depth of my blindness, I say to you: "Things are inside me," this "inside" is an inexact term since there is no actual inside. Things are presented in another way, that's all. I can then play with given space as much as I like. I can even imagine—and if you like, I can do it this very instant—the room in which you are in: I can see to the left the wall and the door. I then try, if I pay close attention, to imagine some people around you, there, sitting and looking. Well, naturally, these would be spatial facts.

But, be careful! Right now, I am playing, just

amusing myself, creating a representation, if you like: a drawing.

If I think of a person, if we right now—go ahead, it's OK—were to think of Georges Saint-Bonnet, who is in Marseilles: Saint-Bonnet is not at all in this particular place. But he is. Not to the right or to the left or behind us. He is inside me, for I have, in thinking about him, the sensation of being located a little lower, even in my physical body, than I usually am. Closer to my heart than my head, I believe, and I'm not being sentimental.

Yes, but in reality, this is no longer a space.

Or instead, it is the only one which counts—that which we have made.

It is that space in which we support ourselves, in which we unite ourselves, in which we envelop ourselves, and, who knows, in which we create ourselves.

Being blind, I have made a certain number of practical observations about these things which I'd like to share with you.

Suppose I am sad. Or embarrassed. I have things which upset me. I am anxious. Armies of small pains race inside my head. I see black butterflies everywhere.

What happens then?

Suddenly I see almost nothing.

When I am sad, walking inside my house, I bump my forehead; I hurt my hand on a half-open door. And I no longer even have a sense of where I am.

This reminds me that I am blind, but blind in a way I don't like. That is to say, in a way which makes me different from others. Also I understand quickly that in order to no longer be blind in the way I detest, all I that I have to do is simply no longer be sad.

What a beautiful Godsend!

It is true that today I think in this clear and peremptory way. At the age of ten, I undoubtedly didn't tell myself things exactly this way.

I know in every case when I am in high spirits, when I am confident, when I observe within myself an air of joy, of life, of peaceful curiosity in regard to things, there are no longer any accidents. I no longer smash my face against objects. I have an impression of knowing them wonderfully well, sometimes of measuring them to the exact centimeter.

In fact, one could write whole books of the newest and most refined psychology on this theme or one like it. But all the books written would add nothing to the experience, which is the only thing that counts. I want to hold myself to that.

There is also what I have discovered when I was impatient. You see this is no longer exactly sadness, though impatience is in many regards a form of sadness. In a word, when I was impatient, I wanted everything to go faster. I wanted to eat quickly. And during this time when I was impatient, all the objects immediately started to turn against me like fretful children. They changed their positions. I could no longer trust them. There was a glass which was on the table, and which I had seen just a moment ago at the tip of my napkin. It disappeared a moment later. It was behind a bottle, and of course in trying to reach for it, I turned over the bottle.

Impatience moves objects in exactly the same way that sadness puts them in shadows, almost eclipses them, surrounds them by some sort of smoke or fog.

Joy clarifies everything.

How many times have I found myself quite simply walking along. And suddenly I receive one of these gusts of contentment, of, so to say, "joy" or "well-being," which is a marvelous feeling because one has no idea where it comes from. There is no known reason. It is as if life were tapping, like rain on a window-pane. One is content. I was content on the sidewalk. Paris became visible to me. I saw Paris. I knew how tall the houses were. I distinguished how wide the streets were. I perceived the automobiles coming and going. And people who approached me had a smell, a history, even before they spoke or I spoke to them. In short, for a brief second, I was all-knowing. I had eyes all around my head, and then, truly, I was no longer blind. It was actually even more than that, in a certain regard.

And it was all because I was content.

Let's look at these phenomena and verify especially their extraordinary positiveness, or rather their material character as opposed to their intellectual, moral, psychic, or social character.

The universe shrinks if I am afraid. It gets gloomy if I am sad. It goes crazy if I am impatient. It becomes clear if I am joyous.

But how does it happen that the universe can be so pliant as that? And then what is the hand which gives itself all these shapes, one after the other? Let's see: If the universe were one reality against which we were obliged to struggle because it was created long before we were, would it not be this way?

If the universe were mere necessity, if it were entirely mechanical, would it be so mobile? Would it allow transformations as concrete in perception as those we get from it?

Why does the universe—which could be a person, ultimately, someone fully adult before we were even born: out there, well-made, well-rounded, definite—why does it allow itself to grow and shrink, to shine forth or to darken its light? That seems almost absurd.

No. What happens, instead, is that we observe ourselves as the hand that manipulates this universe, which gives itself form—though that's an inadequate phrase—inside ourselves.

And we can verify that this hand is not in the objects of the universe that we perceive, but certainly elsewhere.

Thus, during the years following my accident, I lived in a kind of amazement, enchantment, a very beautiful dream.

That expressed itself for me in great lyric expansiveness and in poetry.

Don't worry, I have no wish to speak ill to you about poetry, but that marvel sometimes hid from me something which is more central to all marvels.

I'll try to be a little less obscure.

Having become blind, I had discovered

enchanted worlds inside myself. I think you've felt them as well.

I had discovered enchanted worlds, and I was content with these enchanted worlds, and then, one day I was afraid.

I was afraid because it occurred to me, "Good heavens, what if, by chance or bad luck, I am the author of these enchanted worlds? What if I'm just making them up? If they're just hallucinations that I am entertaining according to some more or less suspicious process, some egocentric compensation for being blind? That would be frightful, because the world would no longer be as beautiful as I have made it, and one day I'll perceive the difference and that will hit me like a ton of bricks."

Then I one beautiful day I recognized that it was not something I had fabricated, but that in fact it had all been given to me.

And given by someone. I say "someone" because that is the most suitable way to say it in words. By someone or something who, evidently, was very much inside of me, but who in another sense was not at all identified with myself.

In fact, I perceived in myself someone who saw all these wonders of the inner life, but who was not me. I profited from it, and then broke it down into parts, transformed it, arranged it, but in the end, it was not I who saw.

I recognized that there was indeed someone watching.

Someone watching deep within.

But this spectator himself did not have a history. And, for him, linear space had no meaning whatsoever.

Who was this someone watching deep within? Imagine for a second that he is identical to the manipulator—the hand—I have just spoken about: to whatever makes the universe expand larger, or shrink, or shine forth or darken. Imagine that he is the same as that. Everything suddenly explains itself.

And everything in fact is explained. There is inside each of us someone watching deep within. Someone who sees.

But whoever is watching is not whoever it is, in us, who sees with our physical eyes—a superficial person indeed—nor even whoever it is, in us, who sees with the eyes of the imagination: that is no longer enough.

He—the someone who's watching deep within —to tell the truth, he sees nothing.

He sees nothing because no spectacles of the inner or outer life interest him. He allows seeing. That's all.

Without him, indeed, we perceive nothing, neither with our physical eyes nor with our inner psychic look. He is more important; he counts for more than anything we perceive.

There is one other thing that I owe, I am almost certain, in large part to my blindness, or rather to which I owe the evidence of my blindness.

Blindness has allowed me to have contact— quite concrete and a good deal closer—with what is going on inside of us all. There are, if you like, whole dull areas of perception that have been elevated, and consequently salvaged.

I have had roughly the best seat in the house at this theater. I have become part of the scenery.

It's up to me to use blindness, to profit from it, to serve it. But in the end, that's how it is.

Yes, you see, when you learn that it is possible to pass beyond your physical eyes, when you discover all that the inner glance can observe, well, you perceive in the end the value of this intimate glance in and of itself. Is it not the essential part of us, something better than anything else? You are no longer content to just be blind once; you want to become blind a second time.

To become blind a second time, why?

And after the second time, a third!

To be blind by accident in the exterior world, in the physical world in one part of its manifestation, is one thing; but imagine also being blind, after that, to all the images of the inner world, to try to look beyond them—beyond the screen of images, in some way—into pure light.

Blind just once? What strange austerity!

There is actually no austerity, for then what we see of the world can never be suppressed, no matter what. Such spectacles indeed will always exist.

It is we, in relationship to them, who perhaps must change.

They will continue to be there, and they will defile us as much as ever, maybe more. And this can also truly be a great fountainhead, a great source for our growth.

Yes, what we see defiles us. One sees these spectacles in their succession, in their interminable progression. But one no longer has to be mixed up with them.

For there is inside of people a kind of glance.

This glance is not at all what one might imagine.

On the level of physical vision, it is carried by what we call eyes, those two organs well protected in the face. Well protected but nonetheless very fragile.

On the level of inner psychic vision, it is carried, if you wish, in a fashion a bit more subtle than on the physical level, but one that is still heavy, mixed up, complex: the power to represent images within ourselves.

But in the end, it's all the same power.

It is never completely exhausted, by either one of these visions.

It is a good deal more central than all that, and a good deal greater. It is up to us to reconcile it within ourselves.

To put it concisely and very simply, when I was eight years old, it was possible to see again, even though I had become blind, because vision is not an organ of the body, nor even an organ of the feeling imagination alone, but an essential power.

A power to help, to assist everything that is, or better yet, to convey in itself everything that is: the power that the spirit possesses to contain the whole universe—our link with the Principle, with God. For that's how it is.

That fountainhead at the bottom of us: I have called it someone watching deep within, also joy.

Perhaps it is exactly the same thing.

And one could almost ask if the only way we have of adapting our senses to the universe, of making better use of them—of seeing, hearing, touching, and sensing as best we can, of not "being blind"—is it not to pray, in the true sense of the term, which is to say to put ourselves in touch with God, as continually and as frequently as possible?

> For this joy is close to you,
> it is in you!
> None of you has a spirit so heavy,
> nor an intelligence so feeble,
> none of you is so far from God
> not to be able to find this joy in Him.
> —*Meister Eckhart*

I even dare believe that interior joy has a secret power to make luck more favorable....

I have often noticed that the things I have done with a happy heart, and with no inner repugnance, have a habit of succeeding happily, even during games of chance, where it is only fortune which rules....

It is useful to have a strong conviction that the things which you undertake without repugnance, and with the freedom which ordinarily accompanies joy, will not fail to succeed well.

Your Highness will allow me, if she pleases, to finish this letter as I began it, and to wish her primarily the satisfaction of the spirit and of joy, as not only as the fruits that one looks for above all others, but also as a means to augment the grace one has for acquiring them.

—*René Descartes,*
Letter to Princess Elisabeth

Against
the
Pollution
of the I

Each morning and each evening I listen, as I must, to news of the war. I must, because I do not have the right to live removed from the realities of my time. And since at present my home is in America, the news that comes over my radio deals with that unnecessary war, that lost war that is being waged with stubborn insistence in Vietnam. But even more often, with ever-increasing frequency, I hear news of a different war: I hear news about pollution. In that war the enemy is not at the other end of the world; he is no stranger, his history is no different from mine, nor is his creed. That enemy is I myself:

he is all of us. Pollution is a civil war. The enemy is none other than the product of our own intellect, the ever-growing number of discoveries made by our practical intelligence. He is our own inventive dreams, the ever new combinations that we assemble out of the sum total of technical possibilities, and whose fallout hews gaping wounds that penetrate deep into our daily lives and affect us even in our most intimate personal concerns. Each day I hear our latest defeats reported.

Where once—why do I say once? it was only yesterday—the Navahos had their peaceful tribal reservation, the Colorado plateau is now poisoned for almost a hundred miles in all directions by fumes from a huge power plant that devours coal torn from the earth all around. Somewhat farther away, the vast virgin forests that cover southeastern Alaska are beginning to be exploited: according to report they are to be systematically cut for lumber. Soon this lung that gave breath to the entire northwestern continent will no longer be able to serve its function. Those were the two latest items from the front in yesterday's news.

Certainly it is good that such news is reported. Barely four years ago it was only a few daring souls, a

few pioneers, who ventured to do so. Now this information (I wish I could say, this voice of conscience)
has become public property. Perhaps now people will
put an end to their madness. Perhaps they will finally sign a "Holy Alliance to Save the Earth." But alas,
this civil war is not restricted to the earth, to the air,
to the water. It rages in ourselves. And about those
battles I hear not a word. I for my part wish to break
this silence. It has already lasted far too long.

Or to put it differently: I come today to share
my concern with you, my very deepest concern. But
rest easy; I am not one of those who enjoy being concerned. I am not one of those who take pleasure in
their own misery, even in their own fright. Together
with you I will be concerned only in the hope that
jointly we may uncover the truths and find the means
that will permit us not always to have to be concerned about the future.

The earth surely is the one field of action on
which this life that has been given us can flourish. We
have blighted it. But this earth is only the lesser half
of our existence, its outwardly visible field of action,
its outer space. There is another sphere for which we
are responsible: our inner space, our *I*. Of this there

is never any mention in the morning news. And yet it is just this, our *I*, whose very existence is being threatened today. So permit me to come to its aid. I will need to be most careful in the battle, for the *I* is the most fragile of all our possessions. But the time for sleeping is past; the time is past even for patience.

Our *I*. That word is so powerful and at the same time so vague that some clarification is called for at the outset.

There are two levels to the *I*, just as there is an outside and an inside to every object, or if you prefer, just as there are two ways in which each of us can approach someone else: in outer appearance, or in actuality as a person. To the extent that there is any willingness at all to speak of the *I* today, one speaks almost exclusively of only one of its manifestations, namely the one in which it appears only as outer surface. This I shall refer to not as the "*I*," but as the "ego."

It is our ego that makes every one of us want to be different from others and, whatever the cost, to distinguish ourselves in some way—frankly, it matters little in what way. Our ego is the desire to gather for ourselves a greater share of the booty of life; to be in the right, even when we are in the wrong. It is our ego that gives rise to those monstrosities about which no one would dream of saying a bad word: jealousy, and competitiveness. It also gives rise to fanaticism, and to authoritarianism that likes to pass itself off as genuine authority. The ego is the seat of that power which seeks to estrange us one from another. You all know the characteristic malady of this century, that so unfortunately has replaced the melancholy of the romanticists: it is the malady of noncommunication. Once we are infected, progressive deterioration is foreordained. The more we are ourselves, the more alone we shall be: so reads the verdict; such is the poison of the ego. We all know it; we even write about it. But what do we do to take up the battle? In very truth, we indulge and gratify the canker in us.

This ego, this treacherous part of our *I,* is everyone's avid concern—and especially that of the educators. In times past, schoolchildren—and even university students—simply were in the wrong when they did not do their work or were unable to understand something. It was their efforts, even their actual accomplishments, that were considered meritorious. Today everyone rushes to protect the pupil's ego: heaven forbid that it should suffer harm! One formulates universally comprehensible truths and facts of middling complexity, so that not a single ego shall ever feel itself inferior. And since each discipline has a point beyond which most egos are unable to penetrate, these limits are set by decree as the end goals of learning.

But that is not all, nor are educators necessarily the most guilty: advertisers have taken possession of the ego. Their entire activity consists of seizing upon isolated whims and, as soon as these have been parceled out to a sufficiently large number of clients, of transforming them into moral truths and legitimate and respected rules of conduct.

What all of them forget is that the ego is not the *I*, but only the most transient, quivering, arbitrary surface of the *I*. By giving the ego free rein, the *I* is put to death.

I told you that the *I* is fragile. It is not even something that we really own, a collection of faculties to which we could point with pride. It is a kind of vitality—yes, at most a kind of vitality. It is a force not far removed from its birth. It is a promise, if you will, given to man, that one day he will be as the universe, that one day he will see the world with eyes opened wide, that he will perceive himself and be

able to recognize that there exists an ordered relationship, a necessary reciprocity between that world
and himself. The *I*, in brief, is still so little that a
mere nothing, as it were, suffices to rob us of it. And
now I see it beleaguered and warred against!

Let us speak of the *I*, the true *I*. At least, let
us try. What I call the *I* is that animation, that
impulse, that allows me to make use of the four ele-
ments, of this earth on which I live, also of my intelligence and of my emotions—yes, even of my dreams.
It is, in sum, a force that imbues me with a power
afforded by no other force on earth: the power to live
without waiting for life to come to me. The ego
needs things, the greatest possible number of
things—be they money, fame, approbation, power,
reward. The *I* makes no such demands. When it is
present, when it is at work, it sets its own world up
against the other world, the world of things. The *I* is
wealth in the midst of poverty. It is vital interest
when all around are bored. It is hope, when all rational basis for hope is gone. From out of the *I* springs
man's whole world of invention. And, finally, it is
what we still have left when all else has been taken
from us, when nothing comes to us from outside and
yet our forces are sufficient to overcome the void.

The *I* of man, it is true, has never been very strong—saving only in a very few isolated individual-ities—and our age is doubtless no more deprived in this regard than all that have gone before. But in our day a new fact must be reckoned with: the attempt is being made to drive out the *I*, to drive it out once and for all so as finally to be rid of it, this peculiar neighbor of ours, this confused indweller within. War is being waged against the *I*, the most dangerous of all wars, because it occurs to no one to declare it openly.

Would you be willing to try an exercise with me? Please do; there really is very little to it! So then let us agree to start today. Tonight, as we get ready for bed, let us stop for a couple of minutes. Two minutes will do; two minutes is a long time to be absolutely still. And let us ask ourselves what actually goes on inside us. What I am suggesting, in fact, is an exami-nation of our consciousness. Yes, but an altogether concrete examination, a physical examination, if I might put it that way. For each of us has an inner space, and we have to cross it to take stock of its con-tents, just as we should have to walk through a room in a house if we wanted to examine the furniture.

What we shall find is a confused jumble of images and sounds; sounds that arise and will not fall silent again, shreds of pictures that never succeed in developing into a complete form. But we shall also find things that are even less distinct, things of the nature of impulses, of stirrings that take on the force of compulsion. All this is no more than the ordinary flotsam of a normal consciousness, and there really is no reason to be astonished at it. But it should prompt us to ask an altogether different question: Those scraps of images and sounds, those fragments of desire—are they really my own? Are they really mine, or have they been instilled in me by others? Is it really my voice that I hear in this way, the voice with which I spoke to someone else just now? Is it the voice of my wife, of my children, of my friends, of a living being? And these pictures, do they bring to mind the things I have held in my hands, the places I have visited, the place where I work? That, surely, is most unlikely. Rather they will be scenes from television (even though I watched for barely an hour); they will be pictures from all the signs, posters, and placards that are thrust under my nose from earliest morning on, in the streets of the town; pictures like the ones on the front page of the paper, in the windows of the stores, even on the box of detergent I bought on my way home. As for the voices, they will be my own and those of my family, but never alone; always they will be mingled with other voices, strangely familiar and yet entirely impersonal— those of all the women and all the men whom I have never met, to whom moreover I would have nothing to say, and who in any case are not speaking to me. What am I saying? Of course they are speaking to me! They do nothing but speak to me—on radio, on television, in the cinema, over the telephone, on paper, on magnetic tape. They speak, yet nothing real takes place when they do. They do not know to whom their words are directed. They speak only because they know that in our day words are a saleable commodity.

My inner space does not belong to me: that is the unpleasant discovery I am forced to make. Certainly I still come across a few personal effects here and there, but rather as one comes across a needle in a haystack. Nor does my inner space belong to these others: I have not consciously made it over to them. It belongs to no one! It is littered with things. We already have automobile cemeteries; I complain about them because they ruin the countryside. And here I am becoming a cemetery myself: of words, of exclamations, of music, of gestures that no one makes quite in earnest, of information and instructions, of word sequences repeated a hundredfold without anyone consciously wanting them.

Granted that I have been preoccupied all evening. I have not paid much attention to the television, and although the radio was on, I was not listening. As for the background music in the cafeteria at lunch and in the elevators, I really could not say anymore whether it was even turned on. And for a long time now I have not had the slightest idea what all the advertisements are about. How, then, could I possibly have been affected? The trap is there, but it has not caught me; at least, I think not.

And yet there can be no doubt that all these noises, all these images flashing through my head, are not my own. My *I* can ignore them; it can look for a way to live without them. But where will it live? All available space is already taken; the outside world has scattered its rubbish everywhere.

This is where courage is called for: the courage to say what at heart we all know, but what we no longer have the strength to affirm. A human being to whom I give the right to speak to me, without my being in a position to reply, is not a human being at all; he is not a human being, but he affects me nonetheless. Music which I have not myself chosen to listen to builds forms within me; it does so even when I am not at all conscious of listening. And these forms are no longer music: they gallop about without order; they shape me without my knowledge. As for all my armchair picture-travelling—from Harlem to Peking, from Suez to Cuba—I did not go there in actual fact, nor did I even want to. On such trips one does not move by so much as a foot; they are and remain utterly useless.

Soon there will not be an inch of our inner space that is not trampled underfoot each day. Love, even love (and who would have thought that love would one day venture out from the most intimate refuge of all?) is becoming a spectacle: the sex act itself is beginning to be performed in public.

All this would not be particularly serious if men were no more than machines. But it turns out that they are really something quite different, for they possess an *I*. And this *I* has its own rules. Or to put it differently: the *I* has certain quite specific conditions under which it will grow. It nourishes itself exclusively on its own activity. Actions that others take in its stead, far from helping, serve only to weaken it. If it does not come to meet things halfway out of its own initiative, the things will push it back; they will overpower it and will not rest until it either withdraws altogether or dies. All this is quite elementary, though objective psychology would no doubt be hard put to prove it. But what does psychology have to do with it? The dying of the *I* is a matter of direct experience. And if the majority of our contemporaries can no longer experience that for themselves, is it not because their *I* has already left them?

The conditions necessary for growth are stringent. They are stringent for all that lives: we have made that discovery with animals and plants, with air and with water. But the *I,* the human *I,* is the most unstable of all our possessions, and the ravages that pollution inflicts on it gain so rapidly that we no longer even identify them by name. Worse, we call them by other names.

Everyone today, for example, respects public opinion—or at least pretends to. We all know that opinion surveys are well on the way to replacing conversation. People are polled on every subject under the sun. But first they are arranged according to social class, age group, profession, place of residence. And then their answers are published, all neatly tabulated by percentages. One day, we may be sure, there will be an opinion survey to determine whether or not people should still get married; and on some other day slightly further removed (but perhaps closer than we think), to establish whether life is still worth living. For people believe in the answers: they really believe. Among those I meet, no more than a handful—one here, one there—have any inkling that statistics are not answers.

A majority, an average—they are not anything real! They are real only for the abstract intellect, which is to say for the manipulation of the masses— by which I mean, for the manipulation of their unconscious minds. For the *I,* they are nothing, hardly worth the computing. If it is not altogether asleep, the *I* knows that truth never consists of what the majority of people do or say. It knows that truth is what appears at the farthest limit of each experience, of those experiences that are lived through personally and to the very end. It knows that the usefulness, the legitimacy, of an attitude does not depend in the slightest on the number of times it has been held before.

It seems to me that we live by nothing but numbers, and that we endow each one with the privileges of a god. What a strange mythology is ours! If only we realized that it is a mythology, and a very primitive one at that!

The average man does not exist. Everyone knows it, and first and foremost the statisticians. Yet it is on this non-man that we lavish the greater part of our care and attention. The other man, the one who is capable of change, the one who could not bear it if he were to discover that he was the average, the one who only says "*I* know" when it is really he who knows—that man suffocates. Each day he is buried deeper under the avalanche of cumulative events. And soon, if we do not set to work with all the desperation due a matter of life or death, the truth will be nothing more in fact than whatever the greatest number thinks, and the good whatever the greatest number does. For once I, who am never one to advocate fear, say: "Let us be afraid!"

Make no mistake about it: war is being waged against the *I*. And just those who have traditionally been closest to the *I*, who have been as it were its guardians and prophets—the intellectuals and the artists—we now see going over by legions to the armies of the aggressor.

Throughout the centuries a writer, a musician, a painter, was someone who expounded a particular point of view to the world. His point of view was his own, and not that of others. It was his own with such intensity and power that at times he was able to find his way back to the realm of the universal. Even the realists, though they might try to make themselves as inconspicuous as possible in the face of the factual world, never excluded themselves entirely from their work. But now, for about the last fifteen years, we see men of creative bent whose express wish it is not only to make themselves as invisible as possible, but to exclude themselves from their work altogether. In place of the *I* there is to be only the act of seeing, only a consciousness to register impressions. Events and even people are no longer to have any relationship whatsoever to the one who sees them or creates them out of his imagination. Is that an honest undertaking? Honest I believe it to be. But can it be taken seriously? Is it conceivable that such an impersonal gaze could be anything other than a concept, an abstraction? When Alain Robbe-Grillet, to take an author from my homeland, writes a novel such as *La Jalousie,* is he unconnected with his story in actual fact, or does he only pretend to be? Is not the mere act of choosing words, of including certain

objects and insights in the narrative while setting
aside others, already a choice and, of necessity, an
affirmation of the author's presence?

But never mind. I have no intention here of
taking up the cudgel against the "*nouveau roman,*"
and moreover every creative venture of the spirit is
fascinating. What interests me much more than the
success or failure of these undertakings is the under-
lying intent. Artists today are afraid of the *I*. They do
all they possibly can do to avoid its being drawn into
the act of knowing. They open the door wide to anything that is not of themselves, anything that in their
view does not belong to anyone personally. I mentioned Alain Robbe-Grillet. We could just as well
think of the American composer John Cage. For his
part, Cage builds structures of sounds of which not
one has been invented, but which are all borrowed
from the domain of outside noises. And today Cage
just as much as Robbe-Grillet commands critical
attention. To be sure, the public does not much like
their work, but it feels that they bring to expression
the essential temper of our times.

Eugene Ionesco and Samuel Beckett go even
further: they stage-manage the disappearance of the
I. Ionesco does so without further comment and, if I

may say so, quite brutally. With Beckett the *I* is dis-
patched no less violently, but its absence takes on
the keenness of nostalgia, the unbearable intensity
of a physical pain. With Beckett, there develops a
metaphysics of *I*-lessness that seems to some like the
promise of a return. Nonetheless, it is a metaphysics
of absence, and not of presence.

Intellectuals by the dozens no longer concern themselves with the content of thought, but
merely with its form. They no longer care about the
connection between the one who thinks and the
things that are thought about, but only about what,
according to them, exists independently of us: about
methods and structures. And that preference has
consequences that can be traced right down into
concrete detail. I see ever-increasing areas of peda-
gogical inquiry in which teachers and students no
longer exist but only a third reality, one that is devoid
of *I*: an arrangement of phenomena, a system.

In short, we are getting ever closer to the
mere object, the machine. We would like to forget for
whom the machine was made—even when it comes
to the mechanism of the universe. We would give
much to rid ourselves finally of that cumbersome
accident, that stubborn unpredictability that is man,

and particularly of that unprogrammable risk that is the *I* in man.

True, the young people protest. For several years now they have carried their protest into the streets. It would seem that they have no love for this world without whimsy, without dreams, without shade, without leisure, without anything that is useless. Recently, and particularly in America, these young people have come to be referred to as a "counter-culture." I cannot help myself; to me, there is an element of salvation in their rejection, even when it takes on despicable forms such as physical brawling and confusion of thought. They have an *I,* and suspect as much themselves. They have not yet been persuaded to the contrary. Perhaps they want to keep it. Perhaps they are better able to do so than we are.

And so there are barricades in all the major cities of Europe, and on the campuses of all the major American universities. In the same vein—and why not?—there is Woodstock and all the "rock festivals" from the Atlantic to the Pacific, and all the way to Provence. But nonetheless I cannot help asking myself, is all this really a manifestation of the *I*?

For if these tens of thousands of young peo-

ple have a real yearning to get to know their inner
needs—the truths that are not for sale and that they
cannot buy—they also, and almost always at the
same time, spontaneously and utterly abandon
themselves to something quite foreign to their *I*. We
all know it: they are hardly off the street before they
have drugs close to hand.

And first in line is that most ordinary of
drugs, which we do not even think of as a poison: the
collective outpouring of emotion. Personal oblivion
lies at the roots of the rock festival. It is staged to
heighten awareness of the moment, to break down
all barriers, to give free rein to the individual impe-
tus for love of others and the joy of being alive. Yet to
achieve these ends it makes use of special incanta-
tions, it glorifies rhythm, it proclaims the anonymity
of the body, and in a kind of exorcism drives out all
individual differences; which is why I fear that such
festivals pave the way for the reign of the "*non-I*." I
have seen joy-drunk hippies in the streets of San
Francisco who were so absorbed in their own bliss
that for days on end they ignored the passers-by
entirely. But their gaze was not turned inward to
their true selves, and their music was escapist in its
relentless monotony.

Owning an *I* is not easy, and keeping it is even harder. Perhaps the search for happiness is not the right approach. And that brings me to the most vexing and urgent problem of all, one that I wish I could avoid, but one about which facts forbid me to remain silent: the problem of the so aptly-named "trip," the drug-induced trip. Into what lands to these trips lead?

I suppose there will be controversy over the degree of harmfulness of the various drugs for a long time to come. If heroin has no chance of passing muster, marijuana for its part has practically passed already. All that is needed, we are told, is to treat it like ordinary tobacco, to make it commercially available and legal. One already hears talk about it in the morning news; not necessarily every day, but at least once a week. I shall not try to resolve that dilemma. I am not particularly curious to know whether or not mescaline results in irreversible addiction. In my eyes all drugs, harsh or gentle, pose the same problem, one that is not at all medical in nature: Is it right to entrust the fate of our souls to chemical substances? Must we rely on sleeping pills for sleep, on herbs for peace of mind, on hallucinogens for happiness? Does that make sense? Is it permissible? And

by that I do not mean morally permissible (for morality changes continually in every way, and most of the
time it deludes itself), but permissible in the context
of natural order. And that is the question I never hear
asked, at least not in official circles.

I understand very well why so many young
people today are drawn to drugs. I understand, you
may be sure, that they want to draw a curtain over a
world in which entire populations or huge forests are
wiped out every day, where persecution is not a matter of passion but of calculated science. And in truth,
how in the long run can we endure a civilization
where the soul is diminished, channeled, labeled,
insulted? How can we find satisfaction in a society in
which fantasy will soon be good for nothing more
than to fill our leisure hours, where everything has to
be weighed—even down to happiness—as cement is
weighed, or fertilizer? I well understand that they are
possessed of only one desire: to get away. But if they
leave, do they ever arrive? They really ought to be
told that they never will arrive!

I had a very dear friend—it must have been
some fifteen years ago. He was a profoundly cultured
man, but he claimed not to be musical. And that
deficiency troubled him. To him music was pleasant

but obscure. He perceived it as an undifferentiated mass whose component parts he was unable to distinguish. One day this man tried mescaline, and while under the drug's influence listened to a recording of Bach's B-minor Mass. Wonder of wonders! From the very first moment the individual voices in the "Kyrie" chorus were there for him to hear, each one separate and distinct. A few days later he told me of his discovery. I said, "Let us try it again, but without mescaline." He no longer heard the individual voices of the choir; he could no longer follow their musical line.

That is typical of the way all drugs work. What they give, they take away again. They fill us with bliss, only to drain us the more dry. With their help we visit far and exotic lands, but when the journey is over we cannot describe them, and we will never take anyone else there. The reason for this is simple: we are not really there ourselves; we left our *I* behind.

All drugs without exception work against the *I*. They set upon it to ravage it. They live through its absence. And that is why, in my eyes, the world of drugs will never be the world of man.

But must we then really be satisfied with the

little we have? For I have not hesitated to admit it: the *I* in us is not strong. It leaves us in a state of starvation. As yet it equips us with only the most feeble of weapons against all that it is not. Truly, we are most poorly armed against the invasion of computations, of matter, of abstraction. But that is just one more reason for not giving up as much as one jot of what we do have of *I*.

Moreover, does it not almost seem that the world of things and abstractions makes use of drugs as weapons against us? What a golden opportunity we would give it if we were to be asleep. Let us imagine (if the thought is not too painful) that human life were divided into two equal parts: one that fell under the dominion of numbers, of speed, of material efficiency, of production, of obedience; and the other in which everyone would curl up and hide, in order then to dissolve away in the artificial universe of drugs. Then the insoluble problem of how to control mankind, how to deliver it into slavery—for which no solution has been found throughout the millennia— would at last no longer exist. It would then only be necessary to lay in the proper supplies. Please excuse this flight of fancy, but it really forces itself on me— to this day I have trouble understanding the policy of

super-arming by the great powers, when an espi-
onage network coupled with indirect persuasion and
a gradual campaign of secret drug distribution would
sooner or later infallibly put the enemy to sleep, and
thus achieve the final object of all war.

I should like to believe that without knowing
it I am being overly dramatic. But I do not think that
I am dramatizing. That germ of humanity in each of
us, our *I,* needs us. Already we have put it out of
mind so as to leave our spirit untrammeled during
the building of the abstract, technological world.
And now drugs drive the *I* out of another refuge, that
of our emotions—no, that is not strong enough: out
of our very soul itself. Sorrow and joy have always
been man's possessions; they have been his exclusive
domain, his pride or his shame. Must we now do without the one and without the other? Shall we turn to
other forces than our own to drive out sadness, to
intensify joy? We are already so fragile; if it really
came to that, we would shatter like glass! I well
remember the report of an American army psychologist concerning American soldiers taken prisoner by
the Chinese during the Korean war—and bear in
mind that this was well before drugs had reached
their present flood tide. These men were subjected

to rigorous brain-washing. Now such diabolical ther-
apy contains without question all that is necessary to
rob even the strongest of their *I*. But what staggered
the army psychologist was the rapidity with which
the captors were able to strip the minds and hearts
of these young Americans of all that made them
American—their belief in their own rights, in their
equality as human beings, even their belief in the
possibility of happiness. I did not find it so astonishing. As human beings, we have all been touched by
the force that we call "the *I*," but it is not riveted to
our bodies. It is at all times ready to give up its place.
It practically cries out for its own submergence by
things, by numbers, by systems, by endless pleasure,
and by drugs. And that is why I say that there is danger, most pressing danger. The *I* is being polluted
even more rapidly than the earth.

It may be that some of you have been won-
dering for some time in the name of what somber
philosophy I harbor such grave fears for the future of
the human *I*. Philosophy has nothing at all to do with
it, you may be sure. I speak from experience; and
before I close I should like, if I may, to recall an
episode from my own life by way of illustration.

In January 1944, together with two thousand
other Frenchmen, I was deported to the Buchenwald
concentration camp. The rules required all our personal belongings to be taken from us immediately on
entering the camp: our clothes, our wedding rings,
even orthopedic appliances. Immediately thereafter
we passed into a second room, where we were forced
to immerse ourselves—head as well as body—in a
bath of Xylol, an extremely strong disinfectant. Then
we were thrust into a third room, where electric
shears hung by their cords from the ceiling. There,
guards meticulously shaved every last hair from our
bodies. Like so many of the measures taken in concentration camps, this one clearly had two interre-
lated objectives: to assure hygiene, and to inflict
humiliation.

And so we passed under the shears in batch-
es of about thirty men. I knew my comrades well, for
we had just lived through three days and three nights
of travel in cattle cars. All were what at that time
were called "political prisoners"—in other words,
men who had voluntarily taken part in the resistance
against Nazism. There was not a coward among
them, not one with any second thoughts. I could
depend fully on their powers of resistance. And yet

suddenly, in the midst of that ludicrous shearing operation, I was stunned to hear sobs. Yes, several of the men were actually weeping. One was a well-known physician, another a baker, a third a professor of sociology—all men very much different from one another. Very different, and yet they wept together, and their tears seemed to say, "Let me keep what I have!"

During the next few days I made it a point to speak with these men. Please don't think for a moment that I held them in contempt! Once one has passed through certain trials in life, one cannot feel anything but loving sympathy towards human weakness. But what had gone on in them? That is what I had to find out. Reluctantly, haltingly, but quite unambiguously, the baker and the sociologist gave essentially the same explanation. Without their clothes, without their hair, these men felt themselves no longer alive. No one would be able to recognize them any more, stripped as they were of their distinctiveness. That thought plunged them into a state of such utter destitution that they were unable to bear it.

But that is not yet the end of my story. The incident that brought these men to tears occurred on January 24th. By the first of March, every one of them was dead. I have to state here that conditions at Buchenwald were very hard. But they were no harder for those men than for all the others. They died—how could I have failed to realize it?—of lack of *I*, of *I*-paralysis.

For two or three centuries now, thinkers have felt themselves entitled to speak of the death of God. Some have proclaimed it as an established fact. I have always looked on their declarations as an ultimate and quite pathetic abstraction. God can no more die than can the *I* of man. So that when I say our *I* is fragile, I mean it in a quite specific sense.

Our *I* is fragile because invariably it diminishes when it is not active. That is not a mere assertion of the intellect; it is a law, and one whose demands we feel more strongly today than ever before. If our *I* gives itself over to anything but itself, it is we who are the immediate victims. We shall have a few moments of heightened pleasure, for there is pleasure also in sleeping; but we shall never again know joy.

And is that not, after all, the true import of those words so many of us use every day: "religion," or in a different vocabulary, "yoga"? The one as well as the other means "reunion," the establishment of a bond. But it most certainly is not enough merely to pay lip service to that bond between the individual man and the universal principle. It has to be desired quite consciously. And if to this day I am beset by fear, it is because I see a steadily growing number of people who no longer have any desire for such a connection. But on the other hand I also remember that this work of the *I*, slow and arduous though it may be and subject to all the pitfalls of the mind and of the senses, is yet the most charged with hope of any that we are able to undertake. And I know that I am not alone in my love of it, nor in my determination to take it up.

Jeremy

The first man on my path is an old man. And you cannot imagine how happy this makes me.

I do not know if there is a greater blessing than to encounter a true old person, that is, one who is joyous. It is a blessing which is rarely given to us, because for most, alas, age is nothing but the blank and degrading addition of physical years. But when an old person is joyful, he is so strong that he no longer needs to speak: he comes and he heals. The one who fills my memory is like this. His name is Jeremy Regard.

It is not I who would give him this name. It was his. How many novelists would like to have invented it?

I would like to be very modest, you know, in describing him, because he was so great and yet seemed so little. He made such a brief passage through my life—only a few weeks—that I can no longer remember his body. I vaguely perceive a man who is vigorous, straight, thickset. Yes, a small man, according to physical measurements. As for his face, I can't see it. I think that I never asked myself any questions about his face, even then. I saw another which was much more real.

I met him in January 1944, in the midst of the war, in Germany, when I was in a concentration camp at age nineteen. He was one of the six thousand French who arrived in Buchenwald between the 22nd and 26th of January. But he was unlike any other.

Here I must stop for a moment, because I have written the word "Buchenwald." I will often be writing of it. But do not expect a picture of the horrors of the deportation. These horrors were real, and they are not pleasant to talk about. To have the right to speak about them, it would be necessary to be a healer—and not just of the body. I will content myself then with the indispensable, the basic scenario.

Sometimes I will even speak of the deportation in a manner which is scandalous for some, I mean paradoxical: I will say in what it was good, I will show what riches it contained.

If I come back to it sometimes, it is because it stands at the very entrance of my life, an attic bursting with pains and joys, with questions and answers.

Jeremy did not speak of the concentration camps either, even when he was there. He did not have his gaze nailed to the smoke from the crematorium, nor on the twelve hundred terrified prisoners of Block 57. He was looking through.

At first I didn't know who he was—people spoke to me of "Socrates."

My neighbors, who were very numerous, pronounced this name which was utterly unexpected in the swarming fear and cold in which we tossed. "Socrates said...," "Socrates laughed...." Socrates was over there, a little further, on the other side of this crowd of closely shaven men. I did not understand why all these people called one person out of everyone Socrates. But I wished to meet him.

Finally one day I saw him—that is, I must have seen him, for to tell the truth, I have no memory of the first meeting.

I know only that I was expecting an eloquent reasoner, a clever metaphysician, some sort of triumphant moral philosopher. That is not at all what I found.

He was a simple welder from a small village at the foot of the Jura mountains. He had come to Buchenwald for reasons which had so little to do with the essential that I never knew them or asked about them.

His name was not Socrates, as you already know, but Jeremy, and I didn't understand why this name wasn't enough for his companions.

Jeremy's tale was that of a welder from a particular part of the world, a village in France. He loved to tell it with broad smiles. He told it very simply, as any tradesman talks about his trade. And here and there one could just barely glimpse a second forge standing there, a forge of the spirit.

Yes, I said "spiritual." However, the word has been spoiled by overuse. But this time it is true and full.

I heard Jeremy speak of men who did not come to his shop just for their horses and their wagons but for themselves. They came so as to go home all steeled and new, to take home a little of the life they were lacking and which they found overflowing, shining and gentle at the forge of father Jeremy.

At this time I was a student. I had hardly ever

experienced such men, they do not fill the universities. I thought that when a man possessed wisdom, he immediately said it, and said how and why and according to which affiliation of thought. Especially, I thought that in order to be wise, it was necessary to think, and to think rigorously.

I stood with my mouth open before Jeremy because he didn't think. He told stories, almost always the same, he shook your shoulders, he seemed to be addressing invisible beings through you. He always had his nose smack in the obvious, the close-at-hand. If he spoke about the happiness of a neighbor upon leaving his shop, it was as if he spoke about a wart, a bump, which had just been removed. He observed things of the spirit with his eyes, as doctors observe microbes through their microscopes. He made no distinction. And the more I saw him do this, the more the weight of the air diminished for me.

I have encountered startling beings, beings whose gestures and words so dazzled that in their presence one had to lower one's eyes. Jeremy was not startling. Not a bit! He wasn't there to stir us up.

It was not curiosity which impelled me toward him. I needed him as a man who is dying of thirst needs water. Like all important things, this was elemental.

I see Jeremy walking through our barracks. A space formed itself among us. He stopped somewhere and, all at once, men pressed in tighter, yet still leaving him a little place in their midst. This was a completely instinctive movement which one cannot explain simply by respect. We drew back rather as one steps back to leave a place for one who is working.

You must picture that we were more than a thousand men in this barracks, a thousand where four hundred would have been uncomfortable. Imagine that we were all afraid, profoundly and immediately. Do not think of us as individuals, but as a protoplasmic mass. In fact, we were glued to one another. The only movements we made were pushing, clutching, pulling apart, twisting. Now you will better understand the marvel (so as not to say "miracle") of this small distance, this circle of space with which Jeremy remained surrounded.

He was not frightening, he was not austere, he was not even eloquent. But he was there, and that was tangible. You felt it as you feel a hand on the shoulder, a hand which summons, which brings you back to yourself when you were about to disappear.

Each time he appeared, the air became breathable: I got a breath of life smack in the face. This was perhaps not a miracle, but it was at least a very great act, and one of which he alone was capable. Jeremy's walk across the quad was that: a breathing. In my memory I can follow distinctly the path of light and clarity which he made through the crowd.

I didn't understand then who he was, but certainly I saw him. And this image began to work inside me until the moment it lit up like a torch. I didn't know who he was because he didn't say.

He had a story which he came back to often: it belonged, he belonged, to the Christian Scientist sect. He had even been to America once to meet his fellow Christian Scientists. This adventure, quite out of the ordinary for a welder from the Jura, intrigued but did not enlighten me. It gave another layer of mystery to his character. That was all. Jeremy, without stories, mattered.

Is it necessary to apologize for using so many images which are linked to simple acts: to eating, to breathing? If I were tempted to do so, Jeremy would prohibit me. He knew too well that one does not live on ideas.

He was truly a manual man. He knew that at Buchenwald we would not live on the ideas which we had of Buchenwald. He said this; he even said that many of us would die from them. Alas, he was not mistaken.

I knew there were men who died because people had killed them. For them there was nothing left to do but pray. But I also knew many who died very quickly, like flies, because they thought they were in hell. It was of such matters that Jeremy spoke.

It was necessary for there to be a man as simple, as clear, who had gone to the depths of reality, in order to see the fire and beyond the fire. More than hope was needed.

It was necessary to see.

The good man Jeremy saw. There was a spectacle before his eyes, but it was not the one we saw. It was not our Buchenwald, that of the victims. It was not a prison, that is to say, a place of hunger, blows, death, protest, where other men, the evil ones, had committed the crime of putting us. For him, there were not us, the innocents, and the other, the big anonymous Other with the tormenting voice and the whip—"the Brute."

How did I know? You have the right to ask: after all, Jeremy said almost nothing about such things. Well, without a doubt, there exist in certain beings, as there existed in him, a rightness and wholeness so perfect that their way of seeing communicates itself, is given to you, for at least an instant. And the silence then is truer, more exact, than any words.

When Jeremy came to us across Block 57, in the midst of his little halo of space, it was clarity which he gave to us. It was an overflowing of vision, a new vision. And that is why we all made way for him.

Above all, do not imagine that Jeremy consoled us. At the point we had reached, any consolation would have been mere romance, a taunting nursery story. We were not in the land of Cockaigne, and if we had been crazy enough to think so for one second, waking up afterward would have been bitter indeed. Jeremy spoke hard. But he did so gently.

There was no trace of glibness about him. He had a mellow voice, precise and deliberate gestures, but this was the habit of his craft, a natural tranquillity. He was a good fellow, I'm telling you, not a prophet.

Jeremy was so little a prophet, he created so little uproar, that I don't know how many, among the dozen men who survived those days of Winter 1944 in Barrack 57, remember him today. I would so much like not to be the only one.

One didn't notice anything special about Jeremy, no sign. He carried the banner of no faith, except from time to time that of Christian Science. But at this time, for me, and for the other Frenchmen around me, this word had only a bizarre resonance.

One went to Jeremy as toward a spring. One didn't ask oneself why. One didn't think about it. In this ocean of rage and suffering there was this island: a man who didn't shout, who asked no one for help, who was sufficient unto himself.

A man who did not dream: that was more important than anything. The rest of us were dreamers: we dreamed of women, of children, of houses, often of the very miseries of other times which we had the weakness to call "liberty." We weren't at Buchenwald. We didn't want anything to do with Buchenwald. And each time we came back it was there just the same, and it hurt.

Jeremy was not disappointed. Why would he have dreamed? When we saw him coming with his immense serenity, we felt like shouting, "Close your eyes! What one sees here burns!" But the shout remained in our throats because from all evidence, his eyes were solidly fixed on all our miseries and did not blink. Even more, he did not seem like someone who takes a great burden upon himself, the air of a hero. He was not afraid, and that just as naturally as we were afraid.

"For one who knows how to see, things are just as they always are," he said. At first I did not understand. I even felt something quite close to indignation. What?

Buchenwald like ordinary life? Impossible! All of these crazed, hideous men, the howling menace of death, these enemies everywhere, among the SS, among the prisoners themselves, this wedge of hill pushed up against the sky, thick with smoke, with its seven circles, and over there across the forest, the electric fences, all of this was just as usual! I remember that I could not accept this. It had to be worse—or if not—then more beautiful. Until finally Jeremy enabled me to see.

It was not a revelation, a flashing discovery of the truth. I don't think there was even an exchange of words. But one day it became obvious, palpable to me in the flesh, that Jeremy, the welder, had lent me his eyes.

With those eyes, I saw that Buchenwald was not unique, not even privileged to be one of the places of greatest human suffering. I also saw that our camp was not in Germany, as we thought, in the heart of the Thuringe, dominating the plain of Iena, in this precise place and in no other. Jeremy taught me, with his eyes, that Buchenwald was in each one of us, baked and rebaked, tended incessantly, nurtured in a horrible way. And that consequently we could vanquish it, if we desired to with enough force.

"As always," Jeremy explained to himself sometimes. He had always seen people living in fear and in the most invincible of all fears: that which has no object. He had seen them all desire secretly and above all else one thing: to do harm to themselves. It was always, it was here, the same spectacle. Simply, the conditions had finally been completely fulfilled. The war, Nazism, the political and national follies had created a masterpiece, a perfect sickness and misery: a concentration camp.

For us, of course, this was the first time. Jeremy had no use for our surprise. He said that it was not honest and that it did us harm.

He said that in ordinary life, with good eyes, we would have seen the same horrors. We had managed to be happy before. Well! The Nazis had given us a terrible microscope: the camp. This was not a reason to stop living.

Jeremy was an example: he found joy in the midst of Block 57. He found it during moments of the day where we found only fear. And he found it in such great abundance that when he was present we felt it rise in us. Inexplicable sensation, incredible even, there where we were: joy was going to fill us.

Imagine this gift which Jeremy gave us! We did not understand, but we thanked him, time and again.

What joy? Here are explanations, but they are feeble: the joy of being alive in this moment, in the next, each time we became aware of it. The joy of feeling the lives of others, of some others at least, against us, in the dark of night. What do I know? Isn't that enough for you?

It was much more than enough for us. It was a pardon, a reprieve, there, all of a sudden, just a few feet from hell. I knew this state through Jeremy. Others knew it also, I am sure.

The joy of discovering that joy exists, that it is in us, just exactly as life is, without conditions and which no condition, even the worst, can kill.

All of this, you will say, came from Jeremy because he was lucid. I didn't say that he was lucid—this quality belongs to intelligence and, in the world of intelligence, Jeremy was not at home. I said that he saw. I have spoken of him as a living prayer.

Subtle people will pretend that the faith of Jeremy was without nuances. Who cares! For him, and for us through him, the world was saved in each second. This benediction had no end. And, when it ceased, it was that we had ceased wanting it, that we—and not it—had ceased being joyful.

These are not great words. And if nonetheless you have that impression, then it is I that am clumsy.

Jeremy was an ordinary man. Ordinary and supernatural, that's it.

One could very well live next to him for weeks
and not see him, and speak only of "an old guy not like
the others." He was not a spectacle in the manner of
heroes or street hawkers.

What was supernatural in him, from all evidence, didn't belong to him; it was meant to be shared.
The spectacle, if it existed, was for us to find and to find
within ourselves. I have the clearest memory of finding
it. I perceived, one day like the others, a little place
where I did not shiver, where I had no shame, where the
death-dealers were only phantoms, where life no longer
depended on the presence of the camp or on its
absence. I owed it to Jeremy.

I have carried this man in my memories as one
carries an image with one because it has been blessed.

And now, how has he disappeared? I hardly
know. Without a sound, in any case, just as he came.

One day, someone told me that he had died.
This must have been several weeks after our arrival in
the camp.

Men went like this there. One almost never knew
how. They disappeared in too great numbers all at once:
no one had either the time or the inclination to look

into the details, the "how" of their death. We let them melt into the mass. There was a solid ground of death in which we all participated more or less, we who were alive. The death of others was so much our own affair that we didn't have the courage to look it in the face.

I do not remember the "how" of Jeremy's departure. I remember only that he came to see me, several days earlier, and told me that it was the last time. Not at all in the way one announced an unhappy event, not so solemnly. Simply—this was the last time, and since it was thus he had come to tell me.

I don't think this caused me pain. It must not have been painful. Indeed it was not, because it was real and known.

He had been of service. He had the right to leave this world which he had completely lived.

I am well aware that people will say to me, "What do you see of the supernatural in your welder? He gave you an example of serenity, at a time when serenity was very difficult to attain. That's good, but that's all. This peace of Jeremy was the result of courage and a strong constitution."

Well, no! We will not have done with Jeremy for that price.

What I call the supernatural in him was the

break with habits which he had completely realized. Those habits of judgment which make us call any adversity "unhappiness" or "evil," those of greed which make us hate, desire vengeance, or simply complain—a minor but incontestable form of hatred—those of our dizzying egocentricity which make us think that we are innocent each time we suffer. He had escaped from the network of compulsive reflexes, and it was this necessary movement which neither good health—or even perfect health, if such exists—can explain.

He had touched the very depth of himself and liberated the supernatural or, if this word bothers you, the essential, that which does not depend on any circumstance, which can exist in all places and in any time, in pain as in pleasure. He had encountered the very source of life. If I have used the word "supernatural," it is because the act of Jeremy sums up to me the religious act itself: the discovery that God is there, in each person, to the same degree, completely in each moment, and that a return can be made toward Him.

This was the good news which Jeremy told, in his turn, and in his very humble manner.

We would all gain a lot by putting memory in quarantine.

The petty memory, at least, the stingy, encumbering memory which makes us believe in this unreality, this myth: the past.

It is this which suddenly brings back—without a shadow of reason—a person, or the shred of an event which then installs itself in us. The image throws itself on the screen of consciousness; it swells, soon there is nothing else but it. The mind's circulation stops. The present disperses. The moments which follow no longer have the force to carry us. They no longer have any flavor. In short, this memory secretes melancholy, regret, all manner of inner complication.

Fortunately, there is the other memory. For me, it is the one to which Jeremy belongs.

This man haunts me, I confess. But he does not haunt me in the manner of the memory. Simply, he has entered into my flesh, he nourishes me, he works to make me live. I spend very little time thinking about him: one could say it is he who thinks of me.

To speak to you of him, I have had to allude to Buchenwald. But do not be misled: Jeremy was never "at Buchenwald." I encountered him there in flesh and blood. He wore a registration number. Others beside myself knew him. But he was not there in the particular, exclusive, individual manner in which we hear the phrase "to have been at Buchenwald."

This adventure of the camp was for him only an adventure: it did not concern him in a fundamental way.

There are people whom I remember only in letting the "little memory" function in me. These people, if I encounter them there, remain there. Jeremy, when he speaks to me, does not do so from out of my past, but from the depths of my present, there, right in the center. I cannot move him.

They are all this way, the people who have taught us something. Because this something, this knowledge, this increase of *presence* in life, they give to us only because they clearly know that they are not the owners. Imagine Jeremy happy as it happens to others to be happy: for personal reasons, due to a history different from that of others, precious and subtle. Do you think that he would still be in my life?

He would have rejoined those picturesque characters, passing figures. But Jeremy was not happy: he was joyous. The good which he enjoyed was not his. Or rather, it was—but by participation. It was just as much ours.

This is the mystery and power of those beings who serve something other than their own provisional personalities: one cannot escape them.

—Translated by Noelle Oxenhandler

*Poetry
in
Buchenwald*

"Hey, Lusseyran! Wait up! Listen!"

The hand of Saint-Jean, thin as a knife-blade, so eager that the bones vibrated like nerves, grabbed my arm. His voice became lower, graver, both angry and tender. He recited,

> I know all sorts of people
> Who are not equal to their lives
> Their hearts are poorly smothered fires
> Their hearts
> Open and close like their doors.

The hand on my arm relaxed, let go, and began gesturing in the air to an invisible witness.

"It's Apollinaire," said Saint-Jean. "Apollinaire! He knew! I tell you, he knew!"

Already my wonderful friend had taken a step away from me. He stood up, lifted his arms. He seemed to have grown taller and to have learned something so essential and so urgent that he had to let me know about it immediately. Yes! It was as though he came bearing news—good news which was going to brighten our wretched lives. I listened to him intently.

I know all sorts of people
Who are not equal to their lives
Their hearts are poorly smothered fires
Their hearts
Open and close like their doors.

He recited the verse again, but with a stronger, more confident voice. This time it wasn't necessary for him to convince me of anything. It had become obvious for me as well.

Now he leaned against my shoulder, as if to make me turn about inside myself and examine the horizon with the new eyes he had just given me.

"Apollinaire wasn't thinking about us," he said. "He was thinking about a prostitute, Marizibill. And yet, Lusseyran—!"

There was no need for him to say more. I let him know I had understood. Or rather—I *saw*. I saw around us the ring of sharp rocks that closed off the road and these men, this multitude of men who were almost faceless and whose eyes open and shut without ever *really* opening. I saw the lines of prisoners who trudged toward the central square to report for work. I saw the cold, the hunger, the fear, all these things that we were not equal to—that were greater than us, too great for us. I knew that the first man I would bump into would not speak my language and would have none of my thoughts. And that for him I, in turn, would be an utter stranger.

As for Saint-Jean, this man who ordinarily asked so many questions, who was so determined to see, to know, to arrive at a simple certainty, a final truth which could sustain him—he gave no further explanations, he sought no further.

I asked, "How did you find these verses?"

"They were there," he said. "I have known them a long time. But it was just then, when I saw the big Russian, a Tartar, and those fifty other Russians who slowly made a circle around him and drew closer in silence and then, finally, threw themselves upon him with cries of hatred and scratched him, trampled him, killed him while nobody did anything or said anything and maybe didn't even see anything.... Then, Lusseyran, I understood."

> I know all sorts of people
> Who are not equal to their lives....

At this my friend made a great gesture with his arm as if to leave unspoken an unbearable thought. This thought had occurred to me in the same instant, and I, too, had found it unbearable. There was this powerlessness of men, our powerlessness, in the face of the events of men's lives, our lives! This was as frightening as the threat of perishing by fire. But Apollinaire had *spoken* this powerlessness. He had known how to say it in such a way that it no longer had the same face. It wasn't any softer, but it was clearer. It began to be reclaimed a little bit, just enough to leave a little room in which to live.

I had loved Saint-Jean for several weeks because he was courageous, ardent, agitated, and especially because he had an unbelievable passion which I had never before encountered to such a degree in anyone—a passion for honesty. He didn't ask himself whether or not it was prudent to be honest in a concentration camp. An honest man is honest in all circumstances. One keeps one's word, one tries to understand, even if it's painful. Inner harmony, moral clarity, these are not things to be sold, even at the price of material security—especially not for that.

I had loved Saint-Jean for weeks, this thin, imperious, and driven man, because he *gave* his human voice, his human resonance, with constancy, from moment to moment, in spite of fatigue, the greatest fatigue. I had loved him from the moment I had entered a detention cell at Fresnes, the evening before the departure to Germany. Then I did not know this man who was speaking in the room of sealed windows. But I had been drawn towards him immediately, and without the slightest impulse to withdraw.

He was not a poet. He was a businessman. For many years he had managed a company in Marseilles very successfully. He had been a member of the Resistance from the very beginning in 1940, and a very effective one: he had set up a repatriation network for Allied aviators. He was not a confused daydreamer. And it was he who had suddenly recited Apollinaire, who had suddenly transformed poetry into action.

Some weeks later—this was in the middle of August—during the time that, unbeknownst to us, the Allied armies were liberating France—I found myself in the same spot. I sat on the little stone wall which faced this long and narrow structure: the basins. A door, several high windows, and, in the interior darkness, a line of big red basins, over which hung a sort of metal mushroom from which icy water hissed. Each morning, the moment the night floodlights went out from the tops of the watchtowers, we were herded here and had to clean ourselves in the dense and sweaty atmosphere packed with bodies.

I was sitting on the wall in the sun, between a young Parisian actor—a frightened and too-beautiful young man with the hands of a woman—and a conscientious and somewhat skeptical teacher from Bourgogne. I said to them,

"Poetry, true poetry, is not 'literature.'"

They both cried out, "Not literature!"

I had surprised, even shocked them. I saw that I would have to explain myself, although I didn't want to. And I began to recite verses, at random, any that I could think of, any that resembled our life at the moment. In a plain, undramatic voice I recited Baudelaire, Rimbaud.

Little by little, another voice was added to my own. I did not know where it came from—I hardly asked myself. Finally, though, I had to listen: the verses were being repeated in the darkness. Voices had timidly joined in behind me, and in front of me. I was surrounded. Without even intending to, I began to recite more slowly.

More men came. They formed a circle. They echoed the words. At the end of each stanza, in each pause, there rose a great hum of the last syllables.

"Keep going! Keep going!" whispered the actor with the hands of a woman. "What's happening is truly extraordinary."

I chanted. It seemed to me in that moment that I knew all the poems I had read, even those I thought I'd forgotten. The circle of men pressed in closer around me: it was a crowd of men. I heard men who weren't French. The echo which they sent back to me was sometimes disfigured—like the sound of a violin with a loose string—sometimes harmonious. The breath of all these men came closer, I felt it now on my face. There were perhaps fifty of them.

I said to them, "Who are you?" The response came immediately, but in a frightening disorder: some spoke German, others Russian, others Hungarian. Others simply repeated the last words of the last verse in French. They leaned toward me, gesturing, swaying, beating their chests, lisping, muttering, crying out, seized by a sudden passion. I was dumbstruck, happy like a child. The noise had grown so loud in a few seconds that I could no longer distinguish a single word. Far from me, behind the oscillating mob, men hailed the passers-by in all the languages of Eastern Europe. No longer trying to understand what was happening, incapable of feeling anything but happiness, a happiness of the throat and breath, I began to recite again. All I had left in my memory was a poem of Baudelaire: "Death of the Lovers." I recited it. And scores of voices, gravelly, croaking, caressing voices repeated, "The dead flames...."

I had a hard time leaving this crowd, escaping from it. I had to throw my arms out and leave, step by step, still reciting. I know that this is hard to believe, but behind me I heard men weeping.

My teacher-friend told me that all these men wore on their shirts the letter "U": Ungar—they were Hungarians.

"But what happened?" I asked.

"We didn't see anything," my two friends said. "They came from all directions all at once, like flies," said the actor with the hands of a girl. But he who usually snickered at the end of each sentence was now serious and sincere.

In the following days I got to know some of these Hungarians. I learned that most of them were Jews who were waiting for what the SS called "transfer to the sky." They all knew they would soon die. I also knew that none of them spoke French, not even a little, but that listening to a man recite poetry, they had thrown themselves upon it as upon food. After a month one of them, Alexander, could repeat without fault the last stanza of "Death of the Lovers"; he could put together all these words which had no sense for him. I asked him what his work was: he was a journalist at Miskolcz, a little village northeast of Budapest.

No, poetry was not simply "literature." It did not belong to the world of books. It was not made just for those who read. The proof of this was growing.

One dark winter morning, in the ink of dawn, we were about thirty exhausted men, shivering, and we were bumping up against each other around one of the red basins for a little icy water. This brutal water, intercepted by a hand, crazed by a face that pressed itself too close, snaked down our naked chests. There was silence, the obligatory silence of all communal activities. But all of a sudden a neighbor began to sing. His voice took off before him and extended out toward us in an immediately magical way. It was the voice of Boris, a man so extraordinary that I can't speak about him just yet. A voice as supple as a head of hair, as rich as the feathers of a bird, the cry of a bird, a natural song, a voice of promise. Without giving notice, Boris had suddenly left this place of cold, dreary dawn and the crowd of human bodies. He recited from Péguy's "The Tapestry of Notre Dame," I think.

Which of us knew what Boris was saying? Who cared? But the thirty of us stayed with our arms held out, leaning forward, a handful of water slipping through our fingers. At last, when the poem was over, a little man whom I had thought for many months was awkward and dull said to me,

"Touch my forehead. It's sweat! That's what warms us up, poetry!"

In fact, the iciness had disappeared. We no longer felt our exhaustion.

One September night, as it was impossible to sleep in the hot and stinking barracks, Sylvain and I stole out and went to the one refuge: the basins. There, there was a little air. Sylvain was a young boy so pale and tormented that he seemed to cry out with each step he took. He had lost all hope, no doubt because being so young, he had not had time before coming to build up enough of a reserve of strength. He watched himself dying, very slowly, gently. He was as patient as he was sad. The hand which he gave me, so stiff it could only open halfway, I could not touch without the greatest caution.

Sylvain was a little Belgian musician. He had been an excellent viola player, and he had been expected to become a virtuoso. But he didn't speak. Of Flemish origin, French by education, he had never really spoken either language. This night I held his arm very firmly, because he was on the verge of collapse. I wanted to tell him about life, this great subject about which he knew so little. As he didn't understand French well, I recited some verses to him. Little by little, as the hours went by, I felt him grow stronger, his closed hands opened. I heard him begin to breathe. Sylvain was no longer afraid.

Poetry is more than simply "literature."

There was one thing that terror could achieve: that hundreds of men seething in the barracks were silent. Only terror and...poetry. If someone recited a poem, all hushed one by one, as coals go out. One hand drew these men together. One cloak of human-ness covered them.

I learned that poetry is an act, an incantation, a kiss of peace, a medicine. I learned that poetry is one of the rare, very rare things in the world which can pre-vail over cold and hatred. No one had taught me this.

A medicine, neither more nor less. An element which, communicated to the human organism, modi-fied the vital circulation, making it slower, or more rapid. It was, in short, something whose effects were as concrete as those of a chemical substance, I was convinced of this.

A student of books, I had loved poetry as I would have loved a phantom: for its unreality! I had thought that it was simply an "art," a great game, a luxury, and always a privilege. What a revelation!

However, not all the poets were found worthy. Some were not allowed in; they were not welcomed by us in our misery. These were invariably the plaintive and lamenting poets.

Lamartine was not taken seriously: he wept too easily, he pitied himself—something we could not take. Vigny took pleasure in complicating life and was too solemn. Musset—he reached us, in spite of his terrifying egoism, because at least he had the art of song. He was an accomplished actor, a magnificent ham.

Hugo triumphed. The least of his verses gave us a charge, a surge of blood. This devil of a man, the irresistible liver of life entered our lives and mingled with us the moment a word of his was spoken.

He could speak of Charles V, the attributes of divinity, an arm around a pretty waist—he always worked on us. There was no need to understand him, even to listen precisely, to listen to the words: it was enough just to let it happen. Life, in his verses, made the chest swell, caught fire, raced forward. It was also a draught of cool wine in our throats—for drunkenness, the benevolent drunkenness which fills up the empty spots, gives one a new life in a place of poverty and pain. We loved Victor Hugo; it was a grand encounter.

Baudelaire also worked on us. But his was a mysterious and cunning power: he had the gift, so rare after all, of finding at the bottom of the darkest holes a little glimmer of light and making it burst before our eyes. He gave meaning to the difficulties of our collapsing bodies. He tied earth back to heaven, linked the real and the impossible—with a flourish that gave us courage. It was permitted, then! Then we, too, were going to do it. In the stolen cigarette, in the crummy pipeful of dried grass, we were going to breathe all the lost paradises. He did it so well.

But the real winners, the tonics, those who worked upon us like a wine, were the poets who sang. I found some in the Middle Ages. Then there were Villon, Ronsard, Verlaine, Apollinaire, Aragon. They surmounted all obstacles. They spoke from another realm. Or rather, it was their step, the rhythm of their gait, which had nothing in common with our cowering. They flew past and carried us on their wings.

Can I remember that this is not just a manner of speaking, that for us these were sensations, that poetry was completely lived by us, and not simply evaluated? We didn't say, "It's beautiful," an expression which only has meaning for those who are happy, the sated. We said, "You see how much good it does!"

I hear skeptics growling, "He's not going to tell us that they were *fed* by poetry." Of course not. We were nourished by a watery soup and a bitter bread. And by hope. Let skeptics not forget this! It was precisely in this matter of hope that poetry acted upon us.

And it was in the thick of these most completely physical, material circumstances which I endured even to the point of suffocation, that I understood how utterly tangible are these things without weight which we call hope, poetry, life.

The little worker from Lens whom I consoled, whom I nourished with the only thing that remained to me on that day, a poem of Eluard, never pushed away this morsel which I held out to him. He never called it "play money." For him it had the most real existence: it was a chance to run, a rope to grab onto. It had a weight in the throat which reached, with one great thrust, towards the future.

To nourish the desire to live, to make it burn: only this counted. Because it was this that deportation threatened with death. It was essential to keep reminding oneself that it is always the soul which dies first—even if its departure goes unnoticed—and it always carries the body along with it. It was the soul which first had to be nourished.

Morality was powerless. All moralities. As if they had been created by artificial conditions of existence: provisional peace, provisional social equilibrium. Ideas, knowledge, could do nothing either: they left despair intact.

Only religion nourished. And next to it, the sensation of human warmth, the physical presence of other human beings. And poetry.

Poetry chased men out of their ordinary refuges, which are places full of dangers. These bad refuges were memories of the time of freedom, personal histories. Poetry made a new place, a clearing.

I met a modest and gentle man. His name was Maurice. I rested near him, because there was no violence in him, not even hidden. Each day he had the same serene expression; he spoke in short, abbreviated sentences. He looked at life from far away, always from very far away. It was as though there was a window between it and himself. Maurice was very sentimental. He was afraid of imposing himself on others. So normally he didn't speak, or else he simply repeated in a solemn way the last words of each sentence of whoever was talking to him.

Maurice had been an accountant in a firm at Saint-Etienne. He had very few memories, but those he had pained him terribly. They all centered around a woman, his wife. I listened to him intensely because it was the first time in months that a man had spoken to me of his legitimate loves and been overcome by emotion.

Maurice had a wife who was not particularly pretty, as he was always repeating, but who was his, who had always consoled him, supported him, and whom, certainly, he would never forget. His voice tightened when he made this promise, as though his return to this woman was forever impossible.

He spoke of Simone's hands, her hair, her heart, her dreams. He spoke of her personality and of her body without the slightest distinction. For him, all of Simone had the same tender and bitter taste.

He spoke to me about her one time, two times, ten times. At last one day I saw that this man was devouring himself. These memories were killing him. "I shouldn't think of her like this," he said. "It's too real. I know. But what can I do?" And one day I thought of poetry. I drew my accountant into a corner and recited to him a poem from Eluard which Saint-Jean had taught me:

> She is there on my eyelids
> And her hair is in mine,
> She has the form of my hands,
> And the color of my eyes,
> She is engulfed by my shadow
> Like a stone under the sky
> Her eyes are always open

And do not let me sleep
Her dreams in broad daylight
Evaporate the suns
And make me laugh, cry, and laugh
And speak without having anything to say.

Maurice listened, said nothing, left. But the next day at wake-up time, he stopped me at the barracks' entrance.

"You know, my friend," he said, "since you told me that poem I haven't been thinking of her in the same way. I see her, but it doesn't hurt anymore. She seems to be everywhere, rather than being at Saint-Etienne. Your Eluard has cured me."

It was true. He spoke so much more loudly, firmly. He was for awhile at least, cured of himself.

I threw myself into a poetry campaign.

In the middle of the block, at midday, I stood upon a bench. I stood there and recited poems. I was the neighborhood singer and passers-by stopped. They pressed in around me. Soon other voices answered mine. I felt them all so close to my body that I could hear the in-and-out of their breath, the relaxation of their muscles. For several minutes there was harmony, there was almost happiness.

Unhappiness, I saw then, comes to each of us because we think ourselves at the center of the world, because we have the miserable conviction that we alone suffer to this point of unbearable intensity. Unhappiness is always to feel oneself imprisoned in one's own skin, in one's own brain. For a few moments there was none of this: the poets, the great poets, spoke the universal, spoke of a world in which all beings exchange strength and weakness, youth and decrepitude.

Simone, Maurice's Simone, was forever no longer at Saint-Étienne. These men and myself were no longer at Buchenwald, and there only, forever. How this helped us to live!

Books were rare, as one can imagine. Some came to us rolled up in food wrappers, crushed in the middle by a hunk of wood. Mutilated books circulated.

And it was thus that one morning the Greek text of the first section of *The Iliad* and a German translation came enveloped by thick spongy rolls of synthetic sausage.

I decreed a mobilization of our memories. I made each man recite whatever verses he knew. Bit by bit I put together poems. I discovered that in men's minds there are great springs of poetry and music which nobody in ordinary life thinks of tapping.

Boris—the one who sang Péguy at the basins—said to me one day, "My child, my child" (as he called everyone he loved). "My dear friend! I beg you to count up everything that is not yours. Your hand is yours, your body is yours, your ideas are yours. What poverty! But poetry, it's not yours. Nor mine nor anyone else's. And that's why it gives us life. Let's not speak of anything else, O.K.? Only poetry, and love."

It is in part because of this experience that I will say without ceasing, "Man is nourished by the invisible. Man is nourished by that which is beyond the personal. He dies from preferring their opposites."

—Translated by Noelle Oxenhandler

And There Was Light

Born in Paris in 1924, Jacques Lusseyran was fifteen at the time of the German occupation, and at sixteen had formed and was heading an underground resistance movement of six hundred young people. In less urgent times this would seem remarkable, but add to it the fact that from the age of eight Lusseyran had been totally blind. Yet *because* he was blind he was able to "see" men, avoiding many potential dangers. "Somehow I became invulnerable," he says, "Then too I became infallible, or nearly...." Nearly.

Told in his own words, Lusseyran's exceptional autobiography shares a life in which blindness and eventual betrayal leading to imprisonment at Buchenwald were gateways, a testament to an inner joy that no conditions, not even the worst, can kill.

Paperback, 328 pages, $14.95
3 Audiocassettes, 270 min., $19.95
(Read by actor/director André Gregory. Abridged.)

call toll-free: 1–800–560–6984
Or send check (plus $4.00 ea. S&H) to:
PARABOLA BOOKS, 656 Broadway, New York, N.Y. 10012
email: orders@parabola.org, www.parabola.org

Other Titles by Jacques Lusseyran

Reviews

And There Was Light, Paperback $14.95

"How do you explain the incredible suspense of this book? You know he lives—he's gone on to write it down after all. So why is your breath caught in your throat and why can't you put this book down even the second or third time through it?" *The Baltimore Sun*

"...thoroughly luminous...Lusseyran allows us to glimpse both heaven and hell on earth through the eyes of someone who has lived through both...even in the grips of darkest evil, Lusseyran is redeemed by light." *The Los Angeles Times*

And There Was Light, Audio $19.95
(Read by actor/director André Gregory. Abridged.)

"...spellbinding...[André] Gregory reads in a beautiful, evenly paced voice which is perfectly suited to the work. The action flows from one episode to the next; the abridgement goes unnoticed. This audio book will touch your soul and light the world around you." *Audiofile*

"Conveys a powerful moment in history, but also reaches further...to deliniate a philosophy of life." *Publishers Weekly*

call toll-free: 1–800–560–6984
Or send check (plus $4.00 ea. S&H) to:
PARABOLA BOOKS, 656 Broadway, New York, N.Y. 10012
email: orders@parabola.org, www.parabola.org